STARTING YOUR OWN BUSINESS

a Consumer Publication

Consumers' Association
publishers of **Which?**
14 Buckingham Street
London WC2N 6DS

a Consumer Publication

edited by   Edith Rudinger

research by   Halina Sand

published by   Consumers' Association
publishers of **Which?**

Which? Books are commissioned and researched
by The Association for Consumer Research
and published by Consumers' Association,
14 Buckingham Street, London WC2N 6DS and
Hodder and Stoughton, 47 Bedford Square,
London WC1B 3DP

© Consumers' Association, February 1983
revised edition August 1986
                   August 1987

ISBN 0 85202 329 4
and   0 340 39599 0

Photoset by Paston Press, Loddon, Norfolk
Printed and bound at the University Press Printing House
Oxford.

CONTENTS

FOREWORD

All at once, it seems, small businesses are news: everyone in Britain is becoming aware of the part they have to play in the economy. Sometimes it can seem (if you read the newspapers) that they will eventually solve most of our economic problems. This has its good side: more government aid, more agencies offering advice and even funds, more courses to teach you how to set up in business (and keep going) are becoming available.

But beware of over-optimism. Your business demands, above all, whole-hearted commitment from you, both psychological and financial, and a great investment in money and labour: having so much at stake, you will also need plenty of courage.

Many people have succeeded: through hard work, perhaps helped by luck. Experience, of course, helps – but even without, many people have leapt into the unknown and landed on their feet.

Unconventional businesses often arise from a person noticing a gap and being willing and able to fill it. You or some member of your family may have said before now 'I wish there were a . . .', or 'if only somebody would do . . . this, that, or the other'. Maybe that is the gap for you to fill.

Whatever business you are thinking of starting, there is a lot to be learned, and a lot of general and specialist information to be gathered. Start with this book.

P.S.
Throughout the book, for he read he or she, and vice versa, for him and his, read her and hers, and so on (except for the bit about maternity entitlements).

HAVING WHAT IT TAKES

To run your own business, of whatever kind, you need not only some capital and some capability but also a certain flair, toughness and some good fortune. Just a very few of the people who start out as small businessmen have enough of both flair and luck to end up as millionaires. You might be one of them; more probably you will succeed in making a living, while enjoying the satisfaction of independence and of doing work you have chosen for yourself.

To achieve this, you must be committed; you must choose a business project that is right for you; and you must prepare yourself as thoroughly as possible before taking the plunge.

commitment

It is no use being half-hearted when starting up a business: you should be motivated positively, not just negatively by a dislike of the job you are in, or unemployment. Your incentive should be to a large extent financial, and do not set your sights too low: from the start, your aim should be to make a reasonable living.

In becoming your own boss, you may find yourself working for a harder taskmaster than any you have had, one who offers unlimited working hours, uncertain holidays, and perhaps, to start with, less money than you were earning before. You will be exchanging the support and companionship of fellow workers for a kind of isolation in which you stand or fall by your own decisions.

There will be few executive perks, or none; you will look at these with a different eye when they have to be paid for out of your profits.

The members of your family should feel equally committed. Their moral support, quite apart from any work-support, will be invaluable, especially during periods of difficulty and discouragement. They ought to be aware that their security depends on your success, that you may have less time for family life, and that the rewards may be some time in coming.

choosing your project

Anyone wanting to start a business has either found a product to manufacture or an idea for one, or has decided to go into distribution, or to provide a service. It is no good saying to yourself 'I want to go into business but I don't know whether to be a manufacturer or a distributor or to provide a service'.

Your choice of business project is a decision you alone can make, because you are in the best position to know what your marketable skills and capabilities are, and which of them you want to be the foundation of your new career.

You may want to capitalise on the knowledge of a trade, the business training or the managerial experience acquired in your previous work. But if it is work that you are or were unhappy in, you may want to strike out in a new direction.

A hobby which has made you an expert at some trade – for instance, cabinet-making, cooking, dressmaking – can be the start of a business, especially if you have already begun to make money by it in your spare time: you will then have the beginnings of a client list, and some idea of a potential market. When you approach a bank or other organisation for a loan, you will inspire more confidence if you already have some history of successful trading. But remember that it is a big jump from moonlighting to making a living from it, and selling a hobby-item to a few friends and relatives may not be a good indication of its appeal to the general public or of its economic viability.

You may have an original business idea. Perhaps you have designed a new product that fills a gap in the market which everyone else has failed to notice; or you may have an idea for a service which would facilitate the workings of some industry.

You may want to enter an established trade by buying a franchise or into a partnership, or by taking over a going concern. But if the trade is new to you, be wary; you are unlikely to be able to master it at the same time as learning the complexities of running a business. Bear in mind that you will be competing with people who are already established experts in the field. It is better to get your training and experience first, by working in the trade for a period, and attending any relevant training courses.

some ways into your own business

If you have developed an original business idea but do not want to deal with the whole of the business side yourself, you may make an agreement with a manufacturer to make your product, retaining for yourself any part of the operation to which you can offer a unique contribution, such as design or marketing. Do not forget that you should, if possible, protect any truly novel idea of yours (for instance, by applying for a patent), before disclosing it to any interested party.

Look around to see if you can find any other small firms, old or new, working in the same or a related field, who might be willing to pool resources with you. For instance, a successful 'merger' of this kind has been achieved between the makers of four-poster beds, piano stools and wooden toys respectively: as well as sharing expenses, they were able to develop a common advertising and marketing policy, while remaining autonomous.

To set up such an arrangement you may have to do a good bit of research to find other firms in your line of trade in your district. Consult your local Chamber of Commerce or Chamber of Trade; if there is a Small Business Club, it will probably be willing to advertise your needs among its members. In London, the London
▲ Enterprise Agency, 4 Snow Hill, London EC1A 2BS (telephone: 01-236 3000) has linked up with six other enterprise agencies to form a national business introduction service, known as LINC (Local Investment Networking Company Ltd).

partial buy-outs

If you have been made redundant by the winding up of a company, consider whether there is any part of the operation or assets (some of the workshop plant, for instance) that you could buy and use in starting a project of your own.

A complete buy-out is a different matter: unless you know exactly why the original company went out of business, and have definite proposals for putting things right, you will not find it easy to raise the necessary finance.

There is little to stop employees who leave an existing company from setting up in competition. Even if there is a clause in their contract of employment restricting their future business ventures, the courts will not uphold a contract that is a restraint of trade and denies anyone the right to earn a living. However, the ex-employer may stop former employees from making use of his trade secrets or confidential information by taking out an injunction.

In making your final choice of project (assuming you have a choice), you should define your field of operations as specifically as possible, and be clear about your ultimate aims. If your ambition is to start up a business in one area and then expand elsewhere, or even to build up a great organisation, you must be sure to choose a business that is capable of such growth. If, however, your sole ambition is to make a comfortable living and sell or close down the firm when you retire, do not choose a business which can only survive by continually growing and expanding.

preparation

The decision when to start will need to be related to the amount of money at your disposal: there is likely to be a period during which you will be paying all the outgoings, with little or no money coming in, while your own living expenses will still have to be met.

Begin by taking stock of your resources and assets, both human and financial. Human assets include your own skills and energy, and those of any member of your family who will be working with you.

Most people starting in business lack one or more of the basic skills needed for success. It is usually cheaper in the long run to buy in a missing skill, say a clerk or book-keeper, than attempt all the paper work yourself unless you really know what you are doing. Not only will you take longer than a skilled person and make more mistakes, but spending the same amount of time in using your own skill (selling, for example) will make more money for the business eventually.

skills to learn

There are certain skills for which you have to pay others that are worth learning, such as typing, elementary accountancy, computer use, administration. If you intend to have a partner, perhaps your own husband or wife, divide up between you who will learn what, at evening classes perhaps, through books or by correspondence course – quite apart from reading around the main subject of your enterprise.

Get used to the idea that, however knowledgeable you may be in your own field, there is a lot to learn. And make sure that you take advantage of the various sources of help: a large number of *Start your own business* training courses are available.

The Manpower Services Commission is responsible for various courses ranging from one week to sixteen weeks. The fees may be paid for and a training allowance given to unemployed people. For details of courses in your area, ask at the local jobcentre, or get
▲ in touch with Manpower Services Commission, Moorfoot, Sheffield S1 4PQ (telephone: 0742-753275).

Ask at your jobcentre or main post office for a free booklet, *Action for jobs*, which includes details of training courses and tells you how to apply for them. It also gives information about various enterprise schemes.

The MSC runs an enterprise allowance scheme whereby people who have been unemployed for eight weeks or more, and are receiving some kind of benefit, may be paid an allowance of £40 a week for one year, to help them set up in business. However, in that year they must find £1,000 of their own to put into the business. Applications should be made at the local jobcentre.

getting advice

Anyone who has previously always been an employee may find that making decisions without any help is very difficult.

Do not be too proud to ask for advice, preferably from those qualified to give it. You may have friends who are professional people – accountant, bank manager, solicitor – willing to advise you, perhaps initially without charging. Or a friend who is already successfully running his own business may be willing to give you the benefit of his experience – provided you are not going to be competing with him!

Although the bank manager is employed to look after the bank's interest, which may not be the same as your interest, it can be helpful to get his opinion, even if he is not providing the funds.

It may take months before you can start. You may need to find premises with all the delays that that involves (including, perhaps, getting planning permission). If your business project is not based on something you are doing already, it is a good idea to make it into a spare-time pursuit while continuing with your job, and getting some experience of the work without burning your boats.

about finance before you start

Whatever your project, you should have a picture in your mind of what stage you intend to have reached in one year's or two years' time, even if you cannot make anything but a very approximate forecast about this. What matters is having a forward plan, against which you will be able to monitor your progress. If things go according to plan, it will give your confidence a boost. And if things are not going as planned, you will be able right away to take whatever action is necessary.

There are some essential basic concepts you must understand, such as overheads, materials and labour costs, unit costs, start-up capital, working capital, short-term and medium-term finance, cash flow, profit and loss account.

The cost of producing anything is made up of a number of elements; how many are involved depends on whether it is a product or a service. Reduced to their simplest terms, they are as follows:

Cost of materials from which products are made: the cost of materials in one year, divided by the number of units of the product manufactured in that year, gives the materials cost per unit.

For a retailer or wholesaler, his materials are his stock of goods. An agent or consultant has no materials costs.

Overheads: generally speaking, these are the standing costs of the business which must be paid whether or not you succeed in making and selling anything.

In the annual accounts, overheads are classified under the following headings:

Salaries and wages	before-tax remuneration paid to office and sales staff, also directors' salaries and any other money they draw out of the business
Rent and rates	

Heating, lighting and other services	gas, electricity, oil, propane gas, water and sewerage, etc
Advertising/marketing	(excluding the cost of any special launch)
Printing, postage and stationery, telephone, telex, etc	all office supplies and expenses
Motor and travel expenses	tax, insurance, servicing and repairs, petrol; expenses of travel by other means
Leasing and/or hire charges	
Insurances	
Professional fees	accountant, solicitor, patent agent
Depreciation	including motor vehicles
Interest on loans and overdraft	rough estimate
Sundry expenses	

Every single one of the overheads costs must be allowed for when you are working out what to charge for a unit of your product or an hour of your time. If you underestimate your overheads, you may find that far from making a profit, you are actually working at a loss.

Direct labour costs: in a manufacturing business, the before-tax wages paid to the people who actually make the product (not the wages of ancillary workers such as sales and office staff).

To find the labour cost per unit, divide the total annual labour costs by the number of product units.

In practice, labour costs should be considered as overheads, since they are fixed: you cannot as a rule hire workers when you have orders for your product, and lay them off when you have none.

costing your products

Estimate, pessimistically, how many units of your product you will make and sell in your first year of full production, given your present resources. Work out the total overheads cost for this period. By dividing the second figure by the first, you get the overheads cost per unit. Thus, if the estimated production is 10,000 units and total overheads are £20,000, you must add £2 to the materials and labour cost of each unit, to break even.

But, of course, you want to do better than just cover your costs, so you add to your break-even figure an amount which will be your profit.

costing in a service industry

The principle is similar, except that instead of charging per unit of product, you will charge per hour of the time spent by a member of your staff in actually doing a job. Overheads usually represent the chief element of costs of the business. If you are, for instance, a washing-machine engineer, or a plumber, your charge for an hour of time should include travelling time and expenses, the cost of tools and equipment, and the wages of the person who answers the telephone and makes out the invoices: all these are overheads. And the chief element in the overheads will be salaries or wages which have to be paid whether or not anyone is actually out on a job. To all this you must add your profit charge. When you do a job yourself, you should also charge for your time, and include a profit element.

If your total overheads costs come to £8,000 for an estimated total of 1,000 job-hours per year, your break-even price per hour will be £8. If you have to replace the washing machine's drum or motor you will have to charge the customer separately for materials.

what is start-up capital?

This is the 'once-for-all' expenditure needed to start a new business, the cash you must lay out before you have manufactured a single item, or dealt with a single client. Unless you start off in your garage with a secondhand typewriter, you will have to pay for some, though not necessarily all, of the following:

○ premises: buying or rebuilding, conversion or even building from scratch
○ plant and equipment, tools
○ goodwill, if taking over an existing business
○ office equipment and furniture
○ installation of electricity, gas, telephone and any other services
○ initial administrative costs: legal and other professional fees
○ stationery: the paper, envelopes, postcards, invoices etc printed with the firm's name
○ publicity: cost of the initial launch.

You should assess this expenditure as accurately as possible and consider ways of reducing it if necessary (for instance, by delaying the buying of any pieces of plant not immediately needed, or by leasing or hiring plant instead of buying).

When you begin to work out how much money you are going to need for your project, you must be sure to include not only the start-up capital (the money needed to get your business going) but also the working capital (the money you need to keep on going in the interval between your outgoings and your receipts).

what is working capital?
In a manufacturing industry, once production starts, some weeks or even months must pass before the products are finished, sold, despatched and paid for. In the meantime, you must keep paying for materials, labour and overheads: the cost of all of these represents your working capital needs.

If you need to keep large stocks of raw materials or finished products or have a number of people on the payroll, materials costs and labour costs will be tied up without, for the time being, any returns. Your working capital will therefore need to be so much the greater. If your suppliers give you 30 days' credit, and your customers pay cash in 7 days (in return for a small discount, perhaps), your working capital requirement will be reduced. At the same time, you will speed up your cash flow, that is, the rate at which money passes out of and into your business. Working capital and cash flow are closely related: the more money you have lying stagnant – in materials, stock, or in customers' unpaid invoices – the more working capital you will need.

In the retail and distributive trades (that is, a shop), where the goods held in stock represent the materials costs, the amount of working capital needed and the rate of cash flow depend on the amount of unsold stock, not so much on unpaid invoices because the retail trade has the advantage that customers generally pay straightaway. A service industry, without stocks of materials or direct labour costs, needs comparatively little working capital: enough to pay overheads costs till the money starts coming in.

short-term finance
As the name suggests, it is money required for short periods of time. It may be needed for start-up capital or for temporary increases in working capital.

If you are setting up a service business or an agency, or plan to be a middleman rather than a manufacturer, you may need little in the way of plant and labour, and consequently a comparatively small start-up capital. But you may still need short-term money, to cover the interval between your outgoings and your receipts.

Such short-term finance can be in the form of a loan for a stated amount, generally with a fixed interest rate and repayment date, or an overdraft. An overdraft usually has a top limit beyond which you cannot borrow; interest is calculated on a daily basis and varies according to the prevailing base rate. An overdraft is usually one of the cheapest forms of borrowing even though there may be a setting-up charge. Its great disadvantage is that it is repayable on demand – though banks seldom do call it in over the short term, as timing will usually have been agreed in advance.

medium-term finance
This is money repayable in 3 to 7 years, and is usually needed as start-up capital to pay for plant and equipment, but it may be working capital. In the past, it was possible to borrow at a fixed rate of interest, but now, with frequent fluctuations in the base

rate, a variable rate is common. The fixed-rate loan, if you can get it, is something of a gamble – you stand to lose if interest rates fall – but it does give the advantage of stability: you know exactly how much you will have to pay for your loan, which is a help in making estimates. It is generally possible to repay a loan before it is due and you must be able to pay off the full amount by the stated date.

WHERE TO GO FOR MONEY AND ADVICE

By and large, money will always be forthcoming for a sound project, well presented. If you cannot get money for your project, either there is some flaw in it, or you have not presented it to the best advantage. If you ask your bank manager for a loan or overdraft on the basis of a few figures on the back of an envelope, you will scarcely inspire confidence.

The obvious source of finance is the bank. Buying money is not very different from buying anything else. Banks make their profits from lending money and they want your business, provided they are sure they will not lose by it. It is best to approach your own bank in the first instance; the manager knows the state of your account, and if you are generally solvent and in control of your outgoings, this will give him some confidence in you. You may get a rapid response: some bank managers take pride in their powers of swift assessment and decision. But if you do not, rather than just waiting for the answer which may turn out to be 'no', approach two or three other commercial institutions.

where the money may come from

If your own high-street bank refuses, try the other clearing banks, any of which may provide the finance. There are also numerous merchant banks able to provide medium-term finance. If your project is closely associated with another country, an approach to one of the country's banks might bring results.

Many banks have developed special schemes for helping new businesses: they include unsecured loan schemes, and loans with capital repayment deferred. It is therefore worth while to investigate various banks as possible sources.

3i
Another line of attack is provided by 3i (Investors in Industry), jointly owned by the Bank of England and the English and

Scottish clearing banks, and using funds from the private sector. 3i invests in viable businesses along the whole business spectrum, from family firms to high-technology enterprises. It helps them at all stages: at start-up, when risk capital may be required; during expansion; and during later phases of development, such as diversification, acquisition, or management buy-out. Where there is a risk element, 3i subscribes for a minority share in the business, in recognition of its role in sharing the risk.

3i Ventures, another division of Investors in Industry, provides both finance and management support to technologically innovative businesses in their early stages.

▲   Contact 3i at 91 Waterloo Road, London SE1 8XP (telephone: 01-928 7822) for the address of your local area office.

BTG

The British Technology Group is a major public organisation offering finance for the development and exploitation of new technology. Its object is to promote the use of new technology in the manufacture of commercial products, particularly where the technology comes from public-sector sources such as universities, polytechnics, research councils and government research establishments.

As part of its technology transfer role, BTG can also offer finance to companies that want to develop new products and processes based on new technology. Through its industrial project finance scheme, BTG can provide up to half of the funds required, and will expect to recover its investment by means of a percentage levy on sales of the resulting product or process. If the project is not commercially successful, the finance will not have to be repaid.

BTG finance is available to companies of all sizes, including subsidiaries. The subsidiaries of foreign-owned companies are also eligible for BTG finance, provided that the resulting business will be located in the United Kingdom.

Where a particular technology requires the setting up of a new company, BTG will consider giving help with the start-up, in return for a minority equity share in the company.

Further information can be obtained from the Marketing ▲ Division, British Technology Group, 101 Newington Causeway, London SE1 6BU (telephone: 01-403 6666).

how to find an investor

There are several agencies which can put the new businessman in touch with people with funds to invest.

▲   LINC (Local Investment Networking Company Ltd.) puts entrepreneurs seeking finance in touch with potential investors who may also have the management skills to put into the business. It consists of six enterprise agencies: Aberdeen Enterprise Trust (0224-582599); Manchester Business Venture (061-236 0153); Medway Enterprise Agency Ltd. (0634-830301); Northamptonshire Enterprise Agency (0604-37401/2); Staffordshire Development Association (0785-223912); Cleveland Enterprise Agency (0642-222836); and the London Enterprise Agency (LEntA), 4 Snow Hill, London EC1A 2BS (01-236 3000). More than 250 other enterprise agencies throughout the country also undertake this 'marriage-bureau' function.

BVCA

The British Venture Capital Association (BVCA) is a professional association of venture capitalists, which also undertakes the function of bringing together potential investors and people in need of business funding. Members of BVCA usually take a minority equity share in a business, and expect to be involved in its management by being represented on the board of directors.

Their names are to be found in an annual directory which gives details of the investing company's preferences as to type of business and its location; the size (if specified) of the minimum investment; the type of financing, e.g., whether for start-ups or
▲ development, or both. Write to BVCA for a copy at 1 Surrey Street, London WC2R 2PS (telephone: 01-836 5702), and then approach individually the companies that seem suitable.

BES

The Business Expansion Scheme has proved successful in attracting investment by individuals into businesses by giving considerable income tax advantages to the investor. The scheme was originally intended to run for only a few years, but is now to remain indefinitely. It applies only to the purchase of new shares in companies incorporated in the UK whose shares are not quoted on the Stock Exchange or the unlisted securities market. The investor must not be an employee of the company nor a partner or paid director of the company, nor a close relative or business associate of a partner or of a paid director. However, the investor may still qualify for tax relief if his total shareholding (alone or in association) will not be more than 30 per cent of the business, or if he is an unpaid director.

Not all businesses qualify. The ones which do not are those for which the Inland Revenue has special rules: for example, financial institutions. Moreover, the company must carry on its business wholly or mainly in the UK, even though it may export everything it manufactures.

The BES regulations are summarised in a booklet, IR 51, obtainable from any Inland Revenue office, or from the Department of Employment's Small Firms Service.

If you are in any doubt whether your business qualifies for the BES, consult your tax inspector or your accountant. Each year the Finance Act (which turns the Chancellor's budget recommendations into law) may alter the workings of the BES in some respect.

▲ A list of approved BES funds may be obtained from the Department of Trade and Industry, General Policy Division 1A, 1-19 Victoria Street, London SW1H 0ET (telephone: 01-215 4901).

other possibilities
Ask any contact you may have in the world of finance – your bank manager, accountant, stockbroker, if you have one – whether they know of anybody looking for an investment. Some people have found investors by advertising in the personal columns of the daily press, but do not hope for too much with this method.

help depending on location
The government has designated certain areas of Britain in which it is anxious to create employment as assisted areas. These are subdivided into development and intermediate areas. Regional development grants, which are only available in development areas, are payable towards approved projects of investment (chiefly in the manufacturing sector), and are calculated, subject to certain limits, as follows: *either* 15 per cent of eligible capital expenditure on new assets, *or* £3,000 for each net new job created, whichever is the higher.

A booklet with full information: *Regional Development Grant: Guide for Applicants*, is available from the Department of Trade
▲ and Industry, ID3A, Room 232, Kingsgate House, 66-74 Victoria Street, London SW1E 6SJ (telephone: 01-215 2574).

In addition, regional selective assistance (RSA) can be made available to encourage industrial or commercial projects which seem likely to do well in an assisted area. Further details can be obtained from the Department of Trade and Industry, ID3A,
▲ Room 230, Kingsgate House, 66-74 Victoria Street, London SW1E 6SJ (telephone: 01-215 2563). The government has also established a number of enterprise zones, and a new business that is set up in one of these may be able to take advantage of certain tax concessions and also rating allowances.

The Council for Small Industries in Rural Areas (CoSIRA) offers advice and also loans to applicants who employ not more than 20 skilled people. The loans are for buildings, equipment and also working capital. The minimum loan is £250, the maximum is £75,000, but the loan is never more than 50 per cent of the cost of the particular project. Interest is payable on the loan at a rate slightly lower than that charged by the commercial market.

In rural development areas, CoSIRA can help businesses to obtain a 25 per cent Development Commission for Rural England grant towards the cost of converting buildings to new job-creating uses. Some of the other services on offer are these: on-the-job skill training in a wide range of trades; help in finding premises; technical building advice, and help with planning permission. CoSIRA's management accountants and marketing officers will advise on drawing up profit plans and marketing plans. CoSIRA also operates joint schemes with some of the major banks, which makes larger loans available.

There are some 30 local CoSIRA offices which help with technical or management problems of the small business in rural areas, also including country towns of up to 10,000 inhabitants. Further information for England can be obtained from the headquarters
▲ of CoSIRA at 141 Castle Street, Salisbury, Wiltshire SP1 3TP (telephone: Salisbury 336255).

In Wales the related body is the Business Development Unit of the Welsh Development Agency, Business Development Centre,
▲ Treforest Industrial Estate, Pontypridd, Mid Glamorgan CF37 5UT

▲ (telephone: 0443-841777); in Scotland, it is the Scottish Develop-
▲ ment Agency, Small Business Division, Rosebery House,
Haymarket Terrace, Edinburgh EH12 5EZ (telephone: 031-337
9595). In Northern Ireland, it is LEDU, LEDU House, Upper Gal-
▲ wally, Belfast BT8 4TB (telephone: 0232-491031). London has the
Greater London Enterprise (GLE), a public investment agency,
managed by 13 London boroughs, which works with the private
sector to generate employment by providing finance and other
support to commercially viable businesses in the London area.
▲ For details and conditions contact GLE, 63–67 Newington Causeway, London SE1 6BD (telephone: 01-403 0300).

In some of the major cities too, local authorities have created
similar support agencies, designed to encourage industry back
into parts of inner urban areas. These are administered by the
Department of the Environment, through the local authorities
making grants or loans to help buy land or renovate buildings, or
to help pay the rent for existing industrial or commercial premises. Some of these loans are interest free.

Some of the grants mentioned here may be taxable, so you
should ask about this at an early stage.

presenting your case
Government help, or local government help, is by no means
automatically available even where such stipulations as the creation of fresh employment are met. One prerequisite in all cases is
that the proposed business must show itself likely to be viable.

In some cases it is stipulated that the presentation of a proposal
must conform to a standard form, which may include an independent accountant's report. Each organisation has its own set of
rules, so the proposal should be written to satisfy these rules. The
information that the funding organisations need, and the way it
is presented, should be very carefully prepared: it is almost a
professional task. It is probably worth involving an accountant at
this stage, if only to help you present a cash flow forecast.

CoSIRA offers help in drawing up funding propositions for
presentation to 3i or to the bank.

The bank itself may help you with a cash flow forecast: all the
major banks run some form of business advisory service, free to

customers, but this help is mainly intended for established businesses. However, many of the banks publish booklets intended for the person who wants to start a business.

Perhaps the best place to go to is one of the organisations whose primary aim is helping the small or new entrepreneur. Amongst these is the Small Firms Service (SFS) of the Department of Employment, whose many (free) publications include *Guide to Enterprise*. You can contact the SFS by dialling the operator and asking for Freefone Enterprise. The SFS also offers a business counselling facility: plans and problems can be discussed with an experienced businessman who is able to give advice in confidence on a wide range of management problems. The first three meetings are free of charge.

In London, the activities of LEntA, the London Enterprise Agency, include a training programme with one-day conferences giving an introduction to the basic requirements for starting and running a business, or an advanced course of four linked weekends. There is also a counselling service dealing with finance and help in presenting a case to providers of finance; it also gives advice on marketing strategy and research, and helps with patents, technical problems, and the commercial aspects of developing an innovation.

The local enterprise agency is a good first point of contact for the small or new entrepreneur, and everyone in the United Kingdom lives within 30 miles of one of these agencies. A directory of the 250 agencies is available, priced £2.50, from ▲ Business in the Community, 227a City Road, London EC1V 1LX; or call 01-253 3716 for the telephone number of your nearest enterprise agency.

Local enterprise agencies are supported by partnerships between local industry and local and central government. They are independent organisations, nearly all run by experienced business people, offering free confidential counselling to people wishing to start a business. They can advise – or, if necessary, suggest other advisers – on problems to do with the sources of finance, and with marketing, planning and training, and finding premises. They may run a number of other initiatives to support local small businesses, such as business training and seminars, small business clubs, and managed small workshop units. 'Managed' means that a manager, who may be employed by the enterprise agency or seconded from a company, attends to the letting of the units and the provision of facilities, and is also available to help and advise the tenants.

But whoever helps you present your case, make sure that you, yourself, understand the calculations, because it is you who will have to explain and justify them to the bank manager or other potential lender, and it will be your responsibility to produce the results to match them. Your forecast must demonstrate, not only that you have coherent and realistic plans for the future, but also that you will be monitoring your progress against them, week by week, month by month, and are unlikely to be overwhelmed by unforeseen disasters.

what the bank manager wants to know

Make an appointment and say why you want to see the bank manager. If you are a customer of his, he will want to look up your banking record before you see him, to assure himself that you can handle your money responsibly. A past overdraft will not be held against you, provided it was by arrangement, not inadvertence. If you are not a customer, he will ask for references from your own bank.

He will want to know what kind of business you want to set up; what kind and size of market you expect to trade in; the likely extent of the competition; how you propose to go about marketing your product. He will ask why you consider yourself particularly qualified for this business; whether you have experience of it, for how long and with what success; and whether you have sought expert advice.

The bank manager will, perhaps surprisingly, want to be sure that you are not asking for too little money. Many beginner businessmen are too modest in their requirements: they do not take account of all the overheads to be paid for, and forget to make provision for slack times in the trade, or unforeseen contingencies, such as a dock strike affecting export business. So, if in doubt, ask for more rather than less.

offering security
The question of what security you can offer is bound to arise. A bank may lend without it, but only on an exceptionally sound proposition, and not always then.

A life insurance policy is unlikely to bring in much if you surrender it to provide capital for your business, but it may be acceptable as security for a bank loan. If you own a house or other real estate, you can use it as security for a loan or overdraft, provided that it is freehold, or on a long lease (over 21 years left, say) but the bank's estimate of its value will certainly be a good deal lower than yours, even after you deduct the amount owing on a first mortgage.

An alternative to consider would be selling your house and moving to a cheaper one, or a rented one, to provide more start-up capital. If you intend to buy or rent a factory from a local authority, especially in a development area, this may secure you a high place on the housing list.

You may feel that to part with the roof over the family's head is too rash, but the people you will be asking for a loan will expect you to carry a portion of the risk. It is important to know that most financial organisations will expect your own stake in the business to equal theirs.

There is a loan guarantee scheme which helps small businesses to raise loans from banks and some commercial sources where a loan would not have been granted without such guarantee. The Department of Employment, through its Small Business Loan Guarantee Scheme, may guarantee up to 70 per cent of a loan of not more than £75,000, but the applicant must be willing to pledge all his available business assets as security for the guaranteed loan, and must already have committed all his personal assets (including his home) to secure conventional term loans or overdrafts. A premium is charged for the guarantee: the premium rate at present is 2.5 per cent per annum of the guaranteed portion of the loan, that is a maximum of 1.75 per cent of the total loan.

Full information about this scheme can be obtained from the
▲ Loan Guarantee Unit of the Department of Employment, Steel House, Tothill Street, London SW1H 9NF (telephone: 01-213 4719/ 3858/5358).

It is very easy, in the desperation of trying to raise capital for a project about which you are very enthusiastic, to give too much security to your source of finance, leaving nothing for future borrowing.

One other point: banks and other financial institutions usually make a charge for setting up a loan arrangement, generally of the order of $\frac{1}{2}$ per cent (negotiated individually in each case). This should be allowed for in one's planning calculations.

The bank manager or other potential lender will want to know exactly what resources you have, which may include redundancy money, savings, stocks and shares and other securities and investments, valuables convertible into cash; and the value of your house and car. He will want to know where the rest of the financing of your enterprise will come from (including other loans, perhaps a loan from a member of the family, at low interest). He will want to know how much you want to borrow, for how long and how you propose to pay it back. He is likely to want to see a budget and a cash flow forecast for at least 12 months which will demonstrate that the loan can be repaid.

cash flow forecasting

At any given time, there will be a difference between your outgoings and your receipts, which has to be covered from funds available in reserve, or by bank overdraft or other forms of credit.

Cash flow forecasting is calculating what this difference will be, based on month by month predictions (or educated guesses) about the times when you will be paying out and when you will be collecting money, over a period of, say, six months or a year.

The outgoings, which are largely predictable, include wages (the payment of which can never be postponed), and materials (remember that some suppliers insist on cash on delivery), VAT (which has to be paid quarterly and is refunded to you quarterly, so it is also a reliable source of receipts) and overheads.

Your overheads will include major bills payable at different intervals: insurance once a year, rates probably twice yearly, rent, electricity, gas, telephone once a quarter. All these will be entered in the books as they are paid, making for an irregular pattern in your accounting, with several bills in some months, and none in others.

receipts
The calculation of receipts is less predictable. The level of sales is likely to fluctuate from month to month. Some customers pay cash in 7 days, usually expecting to be rewarded by a cash discount (negotiated in advance), others pay in 30 or 60 days (also

by previous arrangement). There are bad customers and bad debts, so that part of your money may be outstanding for a long time – or forever: you should allow an estimated sum for this in each month's calculations of receipts.

It is because outgoings are more predictable than receipts that cash flow forecasting is so essential, right from the start: you may have to provide funds for wages, materials and overheads for some months during which there is little or nothing coming in.

The cash flow forecast indicates the actual movement of money, not promises to pay: it is concerned strictly with what comes in and goes out, and the time of each transaction. If you intend to raise capital by borrowing from a bank, the manager will want to examine your cash flow forecast in order to assess your ability to control your financial resources. And your bank manager will also want to see a profit and loss forecast.

how to set up a profit and loss forecast

Start by choosing a target: the amount of sales you think you can achieve in one year's time. Use as the break-even figure the minimum amount you need for your business and personal expenses, and decide how soon you have to reach that point. Not till then is the business moving into profit.

Your sales will need to increase steadily month by month in order to reach the target figure on time. Work out a set of projected monthly sales figures, and arrange them on a 12-month table.

A practical example, using manufactured products to set out the various problems, is that of Bill, a newly-started small-scale manufacturer (but exactly the same method would be used for any other kind of business).

Bill, who is ambitious and confident of his market, plans to achieve sales of £50,000 a month by the end of the first year, so he plans his first year's sales as in line (1) in table A (*opposite*).

VAT does not directly affect the calculation of business profits, so Bill disregards it in this forecast on both sales and purchases.

TABLE A

Bill's projected profit and loss account (*figures in £'s 000, those in square brackets are deficit*)

month	1	2	3	4	5	6	7	8	9	10	11	12	Total	% of sales
(1) sales receipts	1	3	6	10	15	20	25	30	35	40	45	50	280	100
(2) *less* materials purchased	0.5	1.5	3	5	7.5	10	12.5	15	17.5	20	22.5	25	140	50
(3) *less* direct labour	0.3	0.9	1.8	3	4.5	6	7.5	9	10.5	12	13.5	15	84	30
(4) gross profit	0.2	0.6	1.2	2	3	4	5	6	7	8	9	10	56	20
(5) overheads	4	4	4	4	4	4	4	4	4	4	4	4	48	17
(6) net profit	[3.8]	[3.4]	[2.8]	[2.0]	[1.0]	—	1	2	3	4	5	6	8	3

Bill enters in line (2) his cost of materials, which he estimates as a percentage (namely 50 per cent) of sales. He plans to use part-time labour in the first instance, building up to full-time employees as and when they can be justified. His labour figures, again a rough estimate, are expressed in line (3) as a percentage of sales (namely 30 per cent).

By subtracting the labour and materials costs from the receipts, Bill finds his monthly gross profit, in line (4).

In the case of a single-handed owner in a small service industry – say, a plumber – there would be no labour and materials costs, all expenses being charged as overheads, and the sales figures would also be the gross profit figures. In a retail or wholesale business, the materials would be the purchases of stock.

Bill knows that his overheads will vary from month to month; he is doing a one-year profit forecast, and so it is legitimate to average them over 12 months, in line (5).

The resulting set of figures in line (6) is the monthly net profit, and shows him that after the business has broken even at month 6, it is notionally trading at a profit.

Bill realises that if the business borrows money, then the interest charges will reduce the net profit, and he will need to amend the forecast.

He also realises that because he is the owner of the business as 'sole trader' (not a company), he cannot claim his monthly drawings (for his own living expenses) as a salary, that is, as part of the firm's overheads. He will need to discuss his drawings with his bank manager. If he were trading as a limited company, he would pay himself a director's salary, and that would be included in the overheads.

the next step

Estimating profits is, however, only half of the story. The second, and more important half, is being in control of the cash flow. However much profit you expect to be making by the end of the first year, your estimates will be in vain if in the meantime you cannot meet your suppliers' invoices, or your overhead expenses – not to mention the living expenses of you and your family.

how to set up a cash flow forecast

Table B (*on page* 34) shows how Bill works out his cash flow forecast.

He reckons that he needs about £15,000 to buy plant, machinery and office furnishing. He plans to sell his present car (and lease a small van). This, with his redundancy money, means that he has some £7,000 in the bank. He has persuaded his father-in-law to let him have a further £5,000 if it is required, as a stand-by interest-free loan, to be repaid from profits.

He bases his calculations on the same 12-month scheme as his profit and loss forecast, entering his £7,000 in line (8) in the first month. It is personal capital paid into the business.

He estimates his monthly payments to suppliers in line (2): they are the materials costs from his profit forecast, but now including VAT at 15 per cent, and must be paid in cash, as Bill has not yet become credit-worthy.

For line (3) Bill reckons that he can spread his capital payments (for plant and equipment) over the first six months during which he will be building up his sales. He is charged VAT on these purchases.

Wages and salaries (including National Insurance contributions) in line (4) must be paid promptly.

For the purpose of costing, the overheads were averaged out per unit of product, but they cannot be averaged out in making a cash flow forecast: the bills come in and have to be paid at irregular intervals, and this is reflected in line (5). VAT will be charged on some overheads (e.g., advertising, stationery) but not on others (e.g., rent, rates, power). Bill includes the appropriate amounts.

It is obvious to Bill that he will need his father-in-law's loan, so he includes it in line (8).

Bill next goes to line (9) and fills in his sales figures (including VAT), but, as he is giving a month's credit, his first cash receipts come in month 2. He now deals with VAT, currently at 15 per cent, in lines (6) and (10). He totals the VAT charged against the business in each quarter: against this he sets the corresponding

TABLE B

Bill's projected cash flow *(figures in £'s 000, those in square brackets are deficit)*

month	1	2	3	4	5	6	7	8	9	10	11	12	13
(1) opening bank balance/overdraft	nil	[2.04]	[10.42]	[19.27]	[26.6]	[31.1]	[39.1]	[48.23]	[46.88]	[47.15]	[53.35]	[47.88]	[43.38]
PAYMENTS													
(2) suppliers	0.57	1.73	3.45	5.75	8.63	11.5	14.38	17.25	20.12	23.0	25.88	28.75	28.75
(3) plant & machinery	2.3	5.75	2.3	1.15	2.3	3.45							
(4) wages & salaries (inc NI)	0.3	0.9	1.6	3.0	4.5	6.0	7.5	9.0	10.5	12.0	13.5	15.0	15.0
(5) overheads	10.87	1.15	4.95	5.0	0.57	4.30	8.0	1.15	4.15	5.0	1.15	3.5	8.0
(6) VAT office				–			2.25			6.45			9.97
(7) maximum borrowing requirement	[14.04]	[11.57]	[22.72]	[34.17]	[42.60]	[56.35]	[71.23]	[75.63]	[81.65]	[93.60]	[93.88]	[95.13]	[105.1]
RECEIPTS													
(8) capital – Bill	7.0												
– family loan	5.0												
(9) sales	–	1.15	3.45	6.9	11.5	17.25	23.0	28.75	34.5	40.25	46.0	51.75	57.5
(10) VAT office				0.67						–			–
Closing bank balance													
(11) projected borrowing	[2.04]	[10.42]	[19.27]	[26.6]	[31.1]	[39.1]	[48.23]	[46.88]	[47.15]	[53.35]	[47.88]	[43.38]	[47.6]

amounts which he has charged against his customers. But the VAT office (HM Customs and Excise) does not recognise the one month's credit he gives to his customers, so for VAT purposes, Bill must carry back the sales receipt figures to the month before: e.g., the sales credited in month 2 represent a VAT receipt in month 1, in which the goods were invoiced and delivered. In months 1–3, more VAT has been charged against the business than the business has charged, so Bill gets a refund from the VAT office in month 4 (line 10). The case is altered in the subsequent quarters, and Bill has to pass on the excess received to the VAT office, line (6).

Bill now looks at the cash flow month by month. For month 1, the total of payments which is the maximum borrowing requirement (line 7), exceeds both his capital and the family loan (line 8), leaving the business with an overdraft of £2,040 (line 1). He carries this forward as the opening figure in line 1 for month 2. By the end of month 2, the overdraft has increased to £10,420, even with the receipts from the first month's sales. This, too, is carried forward to line 1 for month 3, and so on, month by month. Bill's borrowing requirement, line (11), increases, and at the end of the year, his overdraft is over £43,000, and has been even higher than this for the last five months.

Bill is startled to find that he needs such heavy borrowing to achieve a profit of £8,000 (net, but before interest payments) for the year. This is daunting; he notices that the borrowing drops after reaching a peak in month 10, and this looks to be a promising trend. To check this, he adds a month 13 projection, keeping purchases from suppliers steady at the month 12 level. Alas, he finds that his overdraft increases again. He then looks to see if there are any overheads which he can re-time, or delay paying, but finds that this makes no significant difference to his business.

To improve his cash flow forecast, Bill looks at ways of reducing all outgoings. He accepts that reduced purchases of materials will necessarily reduce sales. He fixes on a less ambitious sales figure of £40,000, but aims for a faster growth in sales, so that he will achieve that figure in month 10, and break even in month 5. By leasing instead of buying some of the plant and machinery he can reduce his capital cash expenditure, but will incur leasing charges, on which VAT is payable. He needs to re-time some of the outgoings, but feels it would be unwise to reduce them all.

Bill now amends his profit and loss forecast, and his cash flow forecast, as shown in tables C and D. Table C shows profits only £200 lower, and table D shows reduced borrowing from month 5, with large reductions in all subsequent months. The year-end overdraft is now £23,650, nearly £20,000 down on his first forecast. He finds that in month 13, the overdraft increases, but is still £18,000 or so down on the original forecast.

The new forecasts, like the old ones, do not provide for interest on borrowing, or for Bill's personal drawings. None of them answers the question: 'When can you repay the loan?' which the lenders are sure to ask. Bill does a back-of-the-envelope extension forecast to month 24: he assumes no changes in purchases and sales, wages, overheads, etc., and ignores inflation. He realises that this is very rough and ready and unrealistic, but still, by showing the cash flow in credit for the last few months, it is a pointer to the sort of term which Bill needs for his borrowing, i.e., 3–5 years, rather than 15–20 years.

Bill believes that the new forecasts can be met, and that they can serve as the foundation of a preliminary talk with the bank manager. After that, they will have to be worked up, probably with professional help, before being presented to the bank or to other possible lenders.

TABLE C

Bill's amended projected profit and loss account (*figures in £'s 000, those in square brackets are deficit*)

month	1	2	3	4	5	6	7	8	9	10	11	12	Total	% of sales
(1) sales receipts less VAT	3	6	10	15	20	25	30	35	35	40	40	40	299	100
(2) *less* materials purchased	1.5	3	5	7.5	10	12.5	15	17.5	17.5	20	20	20	149.5	50
(3) *less* direct labour	0.9	1.8	3.0	4.5	6.0	7.5	9.0	10.5	10.5	12	12	12	89.7	30
(4) gross profit	0.6	1.2	2.0	3.0	4.0	5.0	6.0	7.0	7.0	8.0	8.0	8.0	59.8	20
(5) overheads	4	4	5	4	4	5	4	4	5	4	4	5	52.0	17.3
(6) net profit	[3.4]	[2.8]	[3.0]	[1.0]	—	—	2	3	2	4	4	3	7.8	2.7

TABLE D

Bill's amended projected cash flow (*figures in £'s 000, those in square brackets are deficit*)

month	1	2	3	4	5	6	7	8	9	10	11	12	13
(1) opening bank balance/ overdraft	nil	[4.38]	[8.48]	[19.23]	[26.48]	[28.46]	[30.49]	[39.95]	[36.64]	[32.31]	[39.2]	[30.5]	[23.65]
PAYMENTS													
(2) suppliers	1.73	3.45	5.75	8.63	11.5	14.38	17.25	20.12	20.12	23.0	23.0	23.0	23.0
(3) plant & machinery	2.3	1.15	2.3	1.15									
(4) wages & salaries (inc NI)	0.9	1.8	3.0	4.5	6.0	7.5	9.0	10.5	10.5	12.0	12.0	12.0	12.0
(5) overheads – general	11.45	1.15	5.45	5.0	1.73	2.0	8.0	0.57	4.15	5.0	2.3	3.0	8.0
– leasing			1.15			1.15			1.15			1.15	
(6) VAT office				–			3.96			7.14			8.55
(7) maximum borrowing requirement	[16.38]	[11.93]	[26.13]	[38.51]	[45.71]	[53.49]	[66.70]	[71.14]	[72.56]	[79.45]	[76.5]	[69.65]	[75.20]
RECEIPTS													
(8) capital – Bill	7.0												
– family loan	5.0												
(9) sales	–	3.45	6.9	11.5	17.25	23.0	28.75	34.5	40.25	40.25	46.0	46.0	46.0
(10) VAT office				0.53			–			–			–
Closing bank balance													
(11) projected borrowing	[4.38]	[8.48]	[19.23]	[26.48]	[28.46]	[30.49]	[39.95]	[36.64]	[32.31]	[39.2]	[30.5]	[23.65]	[29.2]

not borrowing but leasing

Leasing is a form of getting medium-term finance without the need to borrow money. The plant, equipment and vehicles you need are bought by the lessor (who may be a finance company) and then leased to you for an agreed rent. At the end of the contract, it is usual for the leased equipment to be sold, and the greatest part of the proceeds (say 90 per cent) will then be returned to you as a rebate of rentals; or you may be able to continue leasing the equipment at a reduced rental.

The lessor claims any tax allowances (such as writing-down allowances) that may be available, and this is reflected in the level of the rental charges, which would otherwise be higher. You yourself can offset the whole rental against corporation tax.

The main advantage of leasing is that your working capital is not tied up in rapidly depreciating machinery and you can reduce your borrowing needs.

The first approach to the lessor generally has to come from you, the potential lessee (though some manufacturers, e.g. of office equipment, practice 'sales aid leasing' – the salesman approaches you fully prepared to arrange a lease). If you are new to the lessor, you may be required to establish your creditworthiness, for example, by providing a bank reference, but usually no security other than the leased goods is required; you may be asked to pay a few months' rental in advance. You have to specify exactly what equipment you want and, if the deal is approved, the lessor buys it from the manufacturer and leases it to you on the agreed terms.

Cars and some equipment (generally office or computer equipment) are leased for short periods and can sometimes be exchanged later for more up-to-date models. You should always try to deal with a lessor who will undertake to be responsible for maintaining the equipment; otherwise, you must be prepared to arrange your own maintenance contract.

▲   The address of the Equipment Leasing Association is 18 Upper Grosvenor Street, London W1X 9PB (telephone: 01-491 2783). You can ask for a booklet *Equipment Leasing* and a list of leasing companies to be sent to you. Most of them are London-based but operate in any part of the country.

Hire-purchase is another way of obtaining plant and equipment without capital outlay. Just as in domestic purchases, you pay a deposit and then regular fixed instalments, and at the end of the contract the goods become your property. The instalment payments are generally higher than interest on a bank loan, but you may not wish to, or be able to, increase your bank loan, and the counterbalancing advantage is that in a hire-purchase agreement the terms are normally fixed, so that the charges cannot be increased if interest rates generally should rise.

looking at the figures

Bill's case has several vital lessons for the new entrepreneur. First of all, you will certainly be surprised when you discover just how much money you are going to need as working capital. It is easy to underestimate one's requirements. Many businesses which are expanding make that mistake: they run out of money because they expand too rapidly. This is called overtrading.

Secondly, an estimated profit margin may appear ample, yet if the volume of sales turns out to be lower than the forecast, the total profits may fail to cover outgoings.

Nearly every first attempt at a profit and loss forecast is too ambitious. That is why a cash flow forecast is needed: to warn the small businessman when his resources are not equal to his ambitions.

It is easy to recast figures at the planning stage in order to deploy one's resources to best advantage, and arrive at a satisfactory and realistic forecast which can confidently be put before a bank or other financial organisation. However, it is terribly easy, when you have produced a forecast you do not like, to adjust the assumptions and figures – in that order – so that it all looks workable. You must look at original assumptions and new ones and see if you are not introducing too much wishful thinking.

why you will need an accountant

If you already know something about business accounting and revel in figures, you may think that you can do without an accountant.

Bear in mind, however, that however nimble with numbers you may be, you are unlikely to have an accountant's grasp of the innumerable regulations relating to taxation or the relevant aspects of company and revenue law, nor his experience in dealing with the Board of Inland Revenue, nor his all-round familiarity with different aspects of business. Here are some of the problems in which an accountant can help you:

- ○ to decide whether to set up as a sole trader, partnership or a limited company
- ○ to find ways of raising capital
- ○ to set up cash flow forecasts and profit and loss forecasts
- ○ to decide whether to register for VAT if you do not have to
- ○ to choose a starting date, and more important still, a trading-year end date
- ○ to keep day-to-day records, account books and ledgers
- ○ to claim all possible allowances and reliefs against tax, and to negotiate with the tax inspector
- ○ to claim expenses
- ○ to cope with pensions, annuities and insurance.

HOW ARE YOU GOING TO TRADE?

You will have to decide whether to trade as a sole trader, in a partnership, or as a limited company. A co-operative is a much less usual business form, but it is also worth considering. There is the possibility, in most cases, of changing to another legal entity later, as your business develops.

Deciding how to trade should be an integral part of your plans, and is something that you should discuss with your professional adviser. There are various considerations, and some which might be significant for your business could be quite unimportant for another.

Perhaps the two most significant general considerations are the question of limited liability, and the fact that a bank or other lender usually prefers to lend to a company.

As to considerations of taxation, what you must do is compare the trading position of a sole trader or partnership and that of a company; and also compare your own position as a sole trader or partner, with your position as a shareholder-owner and salaried director of a limited company. You have to decide what aspects of taxation are most important for you.

For instance, you are obviously not going into business to lose money, but some businesses are likely, in their early years, to make losses which are useful for tax purposes. If you are trading as a company, these losses are carried forward and set against profits in future years. If you are a sole trader (or partnership), you can do this too, but there is also scope for carrying the losses sideways, and setting them against any other income you may receive, and scope for carrying them back to earlier years.

The choice may not be clear-cut, but you should try to assess where the balance of advantage lies. Circumstances may change, so you should periodically review your choice. It is usually possible to change from sole trader (or partnership) to a company without too many tax snags: changing the other way is more difficult.

sole trader

Being a sole trader does not mean that you have to work alone but that you are totally and solely responsible for the business: you take all the profits, but you are also personally liable for all the debts incurred to the full extent of your means. Should you not have the money in the business to pay your business debts, your personal possessions, including your house and home, could be taken in settlement.

Many small businesses start as sole traders and are later turned into limited companies.

partnership

A business partnership is an association of two or more people (up to 20) trading together as one firm and sharing the profits. A single tax assessment is made on the profits of a partnership, so that what is shared out represents post-tax profits. And if one partner should abscond, the others have to pay all the outstanding tax, including what would have been the absconder's share. In cases of losses, all the partners can be held liable for the whole of the firm's debts, to the full extent of their personal means, just as though they were a sole trader.

It is wise, in a partnership, to have a simple agreement, drawn up by a solicitor and setting out each partner's share of the profits, and how each partner's share is to be valued if he wants to withdraw from the partnership, or a new partner comes in and, if one of the partners dies, what should happen to his share.

The agreement should state for how long the partnership is to run or under what conditions it can be terminated. Partnerships that go sour can be messy and upsetting, so it is wise to lay down guide lines of who does what and what should happen in the case of a dispute. Other points that must be agreed are: how much can each partner draw (e.g., monthly) on account of his share of the profit? Are there equal voting rights? Who signs the cheques? What are the arrangements for holidays, and what happens in the case of long illness? What happens if an ex-partner wants to start trading in competition?

All the partners may work in the firm, or there may be a 'sleeping partner' who just puts in money. A partnership agreement can include any clauses specific to the particular set of circumstances.

Sole traders and partnerships may trade under their own name or names, or else under another name or title. However, if the name that you have chosen to trade under is not your own surname(s), you must indicate the name(s) of the owner(s) on all stationery, and display them in your shop or office or place of work.

limited company
A limited company is a legal entity, just as though it were a person, and must be conducted according to rules laid down by company law. They include the maintenance of accounts, an annual audit, and the disclosure of the company's activities to the general public.

The shareholders, of whom there must be at least two, are the owners of the company, but are liable for its debts only to the extent of the face value of their shares. However, a director's liability can be extended by personal guarantees that he may have given to a bank or other financial institution as security for a business loan.

Limited companies may be public or private. If public ('P.L.C.'), the shares are available to the general public and may be quoted on the Stock Exchange. Private companies – the majority – are our chief concern here; they do not offer shares to the public, and style themselves 'Limited' or 'Ltd'.

formalities
In England and Wales, a limited company must be registered by the Registrar of Companies, Companies House, Crown Way,
▲ Maindy, Cardiff CF4 3UZ (telephone: 0222 388588), in Scotland this is done by the Companies Registration Office, 102 George Street,
▲ Edinburgh EH2 3DJ (telephone: 031-225 5774 – new incorporations/ names) and in Northern Ireland by the Companies Registry, IDB
▲ House, 64 Chichester Street, Belfast BT1 4JX (telephone: 0232 234488).

Registration entails submitting a memorandum of association

which must include details of the name of the company, its country of registration, the objects of the company, statement of the limited liability of its members, the amount of share capital and how it is divided into shares. It must be properly signed and witnessed.

You may also submit articles of association (which is something different from the memorandum). They cover a variety of internal matters: broadly speaking, they deal with the rights and powers of the directors and the members; meetings; votes; issue of new shares and restrictions on transfer of shares, such as the right of first refusal for the other members if one of them wishes to dispose of his shares. It is very often easiest simply to say that the standard articles under the Companies Act will apply, and then to list such alterations and additions to them as suit one's particular circumstances.

There are other necessary forms on registration: details of (and consent to act by) first directors and secretary; precise address of the company's registered office; details of stamp duty paid (£1 per £100 value of shares issued); and a statutory declaration that all the formalities have been complied with.

The fees payable on registration are as follows: £50 for a new incorporation; £40 for a change of company name; £20 a year thereafter, for filing the company's annual return with the Registrar of Companies.

It is important to have professional help in registering a company. Some lawyers and accountants specialise in this.

Also, there are company registration agents, through whom you can 'buy' a company off the shelf. The agent has registered the company with stand-in directors, shareholders and secretary, but the company is not operating. When you buy the company, your names are substituted for those of the stand-ins.

If you buy a ready-made company set-up, its name may not be to your liking, but you can change this through the Companies Registration Office.

Your choice of trading name must conform to the rules laid down by the Companies Act 1985 and the Business Names Act 1985 (in Northern Ireland, the Business Names Order (Northern

Ireland) 1986) which are designed to enable anyone dealing with a business to know the owner's name and address. They amount, briefly, to this: the owner of a business must disclose his surname (if it is a sole trader) or surnames (if it is a partnership) or full corporate name (if it is a limited company), together with the address in each case, on the business premises and stationery, if he chooses to trade under some name other than the surname(s) or corporate name. So, for example, if you trade as R. Random; or (Roderick) Random and (Humphrey) Clinker; or Peregrine Pickles Ltd., you are not affected, but formulations such as 'Random's Travel Agency', or 'The Perfect Pickle' will require compliance with the disclosure rules. A complete explanation of these and other rules relating to business names is available in *Notes for guidance on control of business names* from the Registrar of Companies.

co-operative

A co-operative is a business enterprise which is jointly owned by its members. A *worker co-operative* is owned and controlled by its employees; a *consumer co-operative*, by its customers; a *community co-operative*, by the community which the co-operative serves; a *service* or *secondary co-operative*, by the users of the services provided (e.g., a group of small businesses collectively owning and managing their premises).

A co-operative may be a co-ownership, with the workers owning shares in the equity of the business in proportion to their investment in it; or it may be a common ownership, with the assets being collectively owned.

A co-operative may be registered under the Industrial and Provident Societies Acts, with members having limited liability, or it may be incorporated as a limited company. An I&PS co-operative must always have at least seven members, not all of whom need be workers in the business; a limited-company co-operative needs only two members.

Most new co-operatives register either as an I&PS (Industrial and Provident Society) or as a company limited by guarantee, using one of the sets of model rules available from ICOM (Industrial Common Ownership Movement), the National CDA (Co-operative Development Agency) or SCDC (Scottish Co-operative Development Committee Ltd). Model rules make registration easier, cheaper and quicker than having a constitution drawn up, but ICOM provides a 'tailor-made' service on request. Costs vary between the different agencies and the different legal structures.

The registration process takes about six to eight weeks – much longer if any queries should arise. Adopting the model rules, which are already accepted by the Registrar, helps to prevent this.

The essence of a co-operative is that it is run for the benefit of its members and has a democratic constitution: everyone who qualifies may become a member and has one vote, irrespective of the size of his investment. This does not mean that every issue is put to the vote: while very small co-operatives may involve all the members in day-to-day management matters, most of the 1,000+ registered co-operatives delegate these powers to an elected committee, which remains accountable to the membership. Few worker co-operatives employ a paid manager in the conventional sense of the word, but it is common in the other types.

A co-operative must, of course, be commercially viable if it is to survive and compete with other enterprises, and must be conducted on proper business lines. However, when profits are generated, any surplus is generally distributed amongst members in proportion to the extent to which they have traded with or taken part in the business of the society. And though a co-operative may not need to produce a dividend, it must still be able to meet its interest payments and capital repayments on loans.

The principle of co-operation may help to keep the enterprise afloat where ordinary companies would founder. For instance, during difficult trading times members may be willing to reduce their expectations and even make some sacrifices for the good of the whole organisation.

Co-operatives may start in different ways. Most are new-start businesses, but some are formed by workers or members of the community to take over existing businesses, including ones which have failed in the hands of conventional management.

This option, the so-called 'phoenix' co-operative, is by no means simple, and though the attempt may attract much publicity, in most cases it will be possible only if the original business is scaled down considerably before being revived as a co-operative.

New-start co-operatives are created by groups of individuals who wish to combine their skills, or pursue a common interest to create a democratically controlled business; or by members of a community (which may be a geographical community or a 'community of interest') who create a co-operative to provide themselves with a service that they need; or by small businesses which wish to own and manage collectively resources needed by all, such as premises, or marketing.

If you are considering establishing your business as a co-operative, you will need specialist advice. Most areas of the country are served by either a local Co-operative Development Agency, or by local authority officers with specific responsibility for co-operatives. If neither of these facilities is available to you, or you do not know how to contact them, either ICOM or the National CDA will be able to advise you.

getting help
Among the places to go for help or information are:
▲   *National Co-operative Development Agency* (National CDA), Broadmead House, 21 Panton Street, London SW1Y 4DR (telephone: 01-839 2987) and Holyoake House, Hanover Street, Manchester M60 0AS (telephone: 061-833 9379). It was set up by Parliament to promote co-operatives generally; it cannot provide funds, but will advise on setting up a co-operative, scrutinise and assess the suitability of a project, and give advice on raising finance. The National CDA is not directly related to the 100+ local CDAs, which are funded by local authorities.
▲   *Industrial Common Ownership Movement* (ICOM) promotes and advises co-operatives; is a registration agent for co-operative and community enterprises; offers training and consultancy services; has an extensive mail-order catalogue of publications; and provides legal, financial and management advice to its members. Membership is open to all co-operatives, support organisations

and sympathisers. It has a women's section called ICOM Women's Link-up.

▲   *Industrial Common Ownership Finance Limited* (ICOF, 4 St Giles Street, Northampton NN1 1AA (telephone: 0604 37563) administers a revolving loan fund on a national basis for common ownership/ co-operative enterprises. It has specific loan funds for particular areas of the country.

Typical loans are £7,500 over five years at 12% interest. Enterprises which apply for such loans must be able to demonstrate their co-operative status, and also their commercial viability.

The Registry of Friendly Societies gives information and advice about rules and registration. The addresses for different parts of
▲ the UK are 15 Great Marlborough Street, London W1V 2AX (tele-
▲ phone: 01-437 9992); for Scotland, 58 Frederick Street, Edinburgh EH2 1NB (telephone: 031-226 3224); the equivalent for Northern Ireland is the Registry of Companies and Friendly Societies, IDB
▲ House, 64 Chichester Street, Belfast BT1 4JX (telephone: 0232-234488).

▲   *Job Ownership Ltd* (JOL), 9 Poland Street, London W1V 3DG (telephone: 01-437 5511) is a non-profit organisation, whose chief concern is promoting the conversion to worker ownership of existing firms; it also offers advice and encouragement to small new businesses (an initial consultation is free), and has produced its own model rules.

▲   *The Scottish Co-operatives Development Committee Ltd*, Templeton Business Centre, Templeton Street, Bridgeton, Glasgow G40 1DA (telephone: 041-554 3797) offers guidance to groups of people wishing to form a workers' co-operative. Such advice covers all forms of business consultancy and there is now a venture capital company available to provide capital requirements for new and existing co-operatives in the whole of Scotland.

franchises

The principle involved in franchising is basically this: a company which is successful in manufacturing a product or providing a service decides to extend its activities nationally or internationally. Instead of setting up its own company-owned branches, it becomes a *franchisor*, selling its experience and established reputation to individuals, the *franchisees*.

The franchisee contracts to sell the product, or to provide the service, under the franchisor's name and on lines laid down by the franchisor. He has the same choice of business format – sole trader, partnership or limited company – as any other enterprise.

Well-known franchises include fast-food caterers such as Wimpy and Kentucky Fried Chicken, and service businesses such as Prontaprint and the drain cleaning Dyno-Rod. The franchisee buys himself in by paying a franchise fee, the size of which depends on the nature and extent of the business. In return, he is trained to perform the work involved and to run the business. The franchisor may help him to find premises, and will sell him the necessary equipment and materials, for which he will have to find his own financing. The franchisor will require the shop to be fitted out in the style he has chosen to be identified by.

Once established, the franchisee pays the franchisor a continuing management service fee for the use of his name, and for back-up services such as publicity and advertising and product development. This payment may be a management service charge (a percentage of the turnover), or a mark-up or commission on the price of the franchisor's supplies, or sometimes both.

Buying a franchise may not be the cheapest way of starting one's own business, but the support provided by the franchisor may make it the easiest way of setting up.

The cost of setting up a franchise is similar to, or can be more than, the cost of setting up a totally independent small business. But the franchisee buys a commercial advantage through the franchisor's expertise in a specific field and so can avoid many of the pitfalls which often trap the independent small man.

The franchise contract runs for a limited period, say five years, and usually includes the option to renew – not always on the same terms. If the franchisee does not renew, he will be left, when the contract runs out, with just the bare bones of the business – not easy to run or to sell. However, while the contract lasts, the business can be sold as a going concern, provided the buyer is acceptable to the franchisor.

An advantage of a franchise is that the franchisee is granted rights to a particular area – as far as his franchising company is concerned (but nothing can be done to stop other companies in a similar line of business moving into the territory and competing).

It is best to deal with a franchisor who is a member of the British Franchise Association. The BFA has published a Franchisee Information Book (£8 including postage and packing), available from ▲ Franchise Chambers, 75a Bell Street, Henley-on-Thames, Oxon. RG9 2BD (telephone: 0491-578049).

but beware ...

Cowboy franchisors also exist. They charge a relatively high buy-in fee but offer little or no training or equipment. Or the sum involved may be low – about £5,000, say, which is modest by ethical franchising standards – but when you look into what you would be getting for this, you may realise that there is very little tangible return.

The most tell-tale sign of a franchisor who is not above board is that he demands an excessively high franchise fee and management service fee. Ten per cent of turnover is average, though some franchisors may set a somewhat higher rate, in return for providing special facilities for franchisees; but anything grossly in excess of this should be regarded with suspicion.

So before committing yourself, ask the franchising company for a complete list of franchisees and visit one or more existing outlets of the franchisor and talk to the franchisee. Ask, amongst other things, whether the promised advertising and promotional support is being given, locally or nationally. Also try to find out how long the franchisor has been in operation. Whoever your potential franchisor may be, let an independent accountant and/ or solicitor scrutinise the financial data supplied by the franchisor – particularly bank references – and advise you on the proposed contract, including the provisions for termination of the contract.

buying an existing business

If you are thinking of starting up in business by buying a going concern – a business that someone else has started – begin by asking the vital question: why is this business for sale? The reason may be harmless, but there is a chance that the seller knows that the business is under some sort of threat, and is getting out while the going is good.

If you are satisfied with the answer, go on to examine the business in detail. Some of the price of a business is for the physical equipment, and some is for the goodwill, which is the business's ability to keep customers and make profits.

Try to obtain confirmation that the principal customers and also the suppliers will stay with the business when it has changed hands. The seller should sign an undertaking not to compete with you. His existing customers are part of the goodwill of the business, and if he were to take them with him, your going concern would soon be at a standstill.

Check that the equipment is well maintained, in good order, with an acceptable working life before it.

Look closely at the stock: is it all current models? How much of it is obsolete or slow-moving items?

You will be taking over any pending contracts, so check whether the seller has performed them satisfactorily so far, and whether you will be able to complete them properly, and on time.

Ask to see the accounts for several years, and have them examined by an accountant, who will know what questions to ask.

Make a check-list of the further questions that will occur to you as you delve deeper – and insist on getting answers. Try to leave nothing to chance.

are you buying a business or a company?
If the seller runs the business in the form of a limited company, he will have taken advice on the best way for him to sell it, and you may find that he wants to sell it in the same form: not as just a business, but as a company. He does that by selling all the issued

shares in exchange for a single lump sum: you then become owner of the company, and have yourself appointed director in his place.

You may think that this is no different from buying a business in the form of a sole trader: but there is a difference, and it is not to your advantage. When you buy a business in the form of a sole trader (or partnership), it then has a new and different owner (you), and any problems from past years – to do, for example, with taxation or money claim – will still be the seller's problems. You will probably be able to ignore them – unless you choose to settle them, in order to enhance the business's goodwill and reputation.

But if you buy the business as a company, it still has the same owner – the company – and you inherit all past problems, which could involve you in considerable expenditure of time and money.

That is why the apparently simple matter of transferring shares is, in practice, supported by a long, complicated contract which contains, amongst other items, a great many warranties and indemnities in favour of the buyer. But if the seller is later found to have no money any more, these will not be worth anything.

It is wiser, therefore, to insist on buying the business without buying the company. This can be done in the name of your own company (if that is how you want to trade), and the seller should retain the original company.

If he refuses, you will have to decide whether to take the risk, or let the deal fall through.

MARKETING AND SELLING

Marketing and selling your product or service is not just an incidental appendix to producing it: it is the lifeblood of the business.

The two terms are not interchangeable. Marketing covers everything from research, product planning and development to promotion and, of course, selling. Selling is the process of negotiating and carrying out that transaction.

Emerson was mistaken: the world will not beat a path to your house to clamour for your better mousetrap. However efficient it may be, if you do not go to town and seek out people with mice, it will be left on your hands.

In fact, before you started to design it, you should have checked on the mouse population, and the cat population too; it never does to ignore one's competitors.

What is more, when you have found your customers, and are busy with orders, you must plan for future sales. Selling is a continuous process: you should always be looking ahead and planning your marketing strategy for the coming months and years.

The time to start planning for sales is when your product or service is still on the drawing-board. At this point, nothing is lost if you discover that your idea, however good of its kind, will not command a large enough market to make a profit. Perhaps it will be so expensive to produce that its price will be prohibitive; or, perhaps, there are not enough people who long for, say, reproduction antique musical boxes. You still have a chance to rethink it and eliminate expensive labour-intensive processes, for example; or modify it to give it more popular appeal; or scrap it altogether in favour of something else.

Begin by asking yourself some questions:

○ What exactly have I got to offer my customers?
○ Who are likely to be my customers, and where shall I find them?

○ Who are my competitors, and in what way is my product an improvement on theirs or a better alternative (mousetrap v. poison)?
○ What is the best way of making my product or service known to the customer?
○ When do I start planning for the future?

what exactly have I got to offer?

Defining just what it is that you are going to put on the market cannot be done in isolation. You will also have to consider to whom, how, when, and where you are going to sell.

consider your product

If what you are going to sell is something produced by other people, for which you are going to act as retailer or middleman, agent or dealer, you probably have no influence on the actual form of the product. The choice is between one brand and another, between the cheap and popular or the expensive and exclusive varieties of the product.

However, if it is something you have yourself produced, or designed (or had designed for you) and intend to produce, you can decide what the final form of the product will be. You can decide to produce it in several versions, with varying functions and at different price levels; you may make it highly specialised, with only one use, or you may incorporate several functions, in order to widen its appeal; or make it part of a range of related products; or change the materials of which it is made; or scrap it altogether and start again. Do not fall in love with the original idea and insist on going through with it, come hell or high water.

It may be unwise to include every possible refinement right from the start; a highly specialised product may appeal only to a small market. A simpler version may sell better and also pave the way for a more complex one, to be developed now and introduced at a later stage, incorporating new features in response to what were the first customers' reactions. (And if a *Which?* report says that the handle falls off, make sure you redesign it.)

If your product is more sophisticated than the prospective buyers are likely to demand, or too expensive for the ultimate consumer, you must simplify the product or decide to find another market for it, or produce two varieties for different types of user.

If the product requires the skills of several craftsmen, for example cabinet-maker and precision engineer, make sure from the start that you will have a supply of skilled labour to depend on. It is no use building up a market for a product if you cannot maintain the supply. It might be better to design something that can be made by less skilled labour.

Ask yourself if the demand for your product is likely to be seasonal. A new nutcracker, for example, however super-efficient, is likely to sell readily only in the period before Christmas, so you may need another product (or several) to keep your plant and labour occupied for the rest of the year.

Where what you have to sell is quite simply a service plus your expertise, the need to define it precisely applies just as much as to a product. If, for example, you are setting up a security business, you should decide whether you are best able to supply a delivery service (complete with armoured cars), or human guards, or guard dogs, or specialist advice on how people can improve the security of their house or factory.

In the case of a consultancy or agency, too, define your scope as closely as possible, and relate it to your own experience. Rather than grandly planning to become an import-export agent, aim to trade with particular geographical areas and in specific products, preferably areas and products with which you are already familiar. When setting up as a consultant, you are more likely to succeed if you closely limit your field to where your particular expertise lies. Do not wait for your clients' reactions to tell you on what topics you are not qualified to give advice.

who are my customers and where shall I find them?
The nature of the product or service will dictate a general answer: woollen sweaters are for people, automated filing systems are for offices, easy-to-install damp-proof window frames should

interest the building industry and the d-i-y- enthusiast. A solar-panel water heating system may have limited use in England, but could be the basis of an export trade with sun-drenched countries.

Next, get some notion of how you should sell your products to your prospective customers, whether through a retail shop or a department store, through a wholesaler or by mail order, through agents or directly, in the UK or abroad.

some market research
Researching your market is not as formidable as it sounds. You yourself can do a lot of 'market research' from sources ready to hand, starting with public libraries.

The central library in your area should have a comprehensive reference department. In the commercial section of this you will find trade directories and publications relating to your business; Yellow Pages and telephone directories covering the whole country; directories of foreign importers; official digests of statistics, and much else.

Londoners are lucky: they command the superb resources of the Central Reference Library's commercial and technical section, but the chief town or city in your area should offer comparable facilities.

The Government Statistical Service makes available, on demand, a vast amount of information gathered by government departments, and by the Business Statistics Office and the Office of Population Censuses and Surveys. The booklet *Government Statistics: A Brief Guide to Sources*, available free from the Information Services Division, Cabinet Office (CSO), Great George Street, London SW1P 3AQ (telephone: 01-270 6363/6364), lists the various kinds of facts and figures available, and relates them to different aspects of business, such as marketing; the retail trade; external trade. Much of this is published in a series called *Business Monitors*.

Someone planning a comprehensive marketing strategy may want to study figures relating to national income and expenditure and population trends and projections. This may sound grandiose; what it amounts to is that you might get an idea of what proportion of what kind of people (teenagers, pensioners) is likely to want your product.

Some examples of where to find useful facts and figures include: *Classified List of Manufacturing Businesses* (issued in 10 parts), *Quarterly Statistics of Manufacturers' Sales*, *Population Trends* (quarterly), *Family Expenditure Survey* (annual), *Overseas Trade Statistics of the United Kingdom* (monthly), *Annual Statistics on Retail Traders*. You can ask for them at the public library; they are rather expensive.

Useful free publications, such as *Marketing: A Guide For Small Firms; How To Start Exporting; Selling To Large Firms* are available from the Small Firms Service of the Department of Employment. To find out the address of your nearest small business centre, from which you can get much valuable information, dial 100 and ask the operator for Freefone Enterprise.

trade organisations, trade journals, trade exhibitions
As a learner, you should snatch at every opportunity of consulting those who are already experts: your own trade organisation should be able to help you. Trade associations are listed in the Directory of British Associations (available in reference libraries). Journals and exhibitions will inform you about the prospects of your trade, future developments and new products, and will give you an idea who some of your potential buyers might be. The *Financial Times* publishes the dates and venues of forthcoming trade exhibitions. So, of course, does the *Exhibition Bulletin* (266 ▲ Kirkdale, Sydenham, London SE26 4RZ; telephone: 01-778 2288): the information it offers is world-wide in scope and two years or more in advance, which makes planning ahead easier.

If your product is to be sold to some trade or industry, you can use its trade directories to compile a list of potential customers.

You may find details of some more relevant journals and publications by looking at Brads Media Lists which are categorised by subject.

Chambers of Commerce and Chambers of Trade, besides being a source of information, may allow you access to their libraries.

Wherever economics or business studies are taught, at universities, polytechnics, local technical colleges, schools of business studies, you should be able to find a library, experts to consult, even students willing, for a modest fee, to do your market research for you. Make the arrangement, preferably in the autumn term, through the Management Studies or Trading Department.

dry run
If you have started to manufacture your product in your spare time and are wondering whether to go into full production, try to test your market. This can be done for a small outlay, perhaps by distributing a few hundred leaflets, or putting a couple of dozen cards in shop windows. Do not distribute too many leaflets at a time, in case you would then not be able to deal with the number of requests. Space out the distribution. This should give you some idea of whether anyone in the district is interested in what you have to offer.

who are my competitors?

The Yellow Pages will tell you what other similar businesses there are in your area, if you are counting on local trade.

Make yourself familiar with your competitors' products. Watch particularly for competitors' publicity and advertising: yours will have to be different and better. Send for their promotional literature and price lists, attend trade exhibitions. Trade directories and the trade press will give you relevant addresses.

If yours is a service industry, try approaching a similar firm for advice. You may find one operating in another area remarkably willing to show you round the premises and answer questions. But do not expect your local firms to welcome and train more competition, and do not, in your enthusiasm, give your ideas away to someone who may beat you to it.

If the competitor's product is sold through retail outlets, go and see it at the point of sale to find out how it is displayed and promoted.

The object is to find out how your product would compare. Has it any unique features? Why should people prefer it to any other? What special features have the other products got, that could be incorporated in your product (with due regard to infringement of copyright or patents)? Something as simple as a hook, a lid, a heatproof base, could make all the difference to the appeal of a gadget.

how do I sell my products?

The actual business of putting anything on the market has several aspects including advertising, sales and distribution, pricing.

advertising and promotion

Which of the various media you should use will depend very much on the nature of your product (or service), and how much you can afford to spend on making it known.

The local press is particularly suited to a service or business which relies on local customers such as a plumber, electrician, hairdresser, launderette, flower shop. The cheapest advertisement is an insert in the classified advertisement section. This kind of advertisement does not catch the eye: it simply waits for someone looking for that type of service or product. So, to be effective, it should appear regularly.

If you want to catch the reader's passing glance, a display advertisement will be more effective or, if your budget permits, a larger, specially designed advertisement, placed on an editorial page (perhaps with a coupon on which further information can be requested, but then the return postage must be budgeted for). Such an advertisement, too, should appear regularly. A coupon is most effective when placed on the outside edge of the page, where it is easy to cut out.

Many local papers undertake the design of a display advertisement but a professionally designed one is likely to be more eye catching. You can find a graphic designer through the Yellow Pages, but before commissioning him or her, make sure you know the cost.

Advertising in national newspapers and magazines is suited to a firm hoping to sell by mail order. It is essential to choose publications that are right for the type of goods – women's clothing in women's pages and magazines, sets of spanners in do-it-yourself magazines.

The trade press is the medium for goods that are sold not to individual consumers but to other firms. Much the same considerations apply as in the case of the national press; and where your advertisement is likely to appear cheek-by-jowl with those of competitors, it is essential to have an effective display that stands out, so professional advice is indicated. There are plenty of small local advertising agencies whose names can be found in the Yellow Pages or obtained from the Institute of Practitioners in ▲ Advertising (IPA), 44 Belgrave Square, London SW1X 8QX (telephone: 01-235 7020). Ask to see specimens of work and get an estimate before you engage one.

What you will be paying for is know-how – an agency should be able to design your advertising, advise on its content and wording, and place it in the appropriate media at the right times.

Trade exhibitions and local trade fairs have a triple function – for market research, for finding out what your competitors are producing, and also for selling your own goods to firms. They are not usually open to the general public. Your trade press will tell you where and when appropriate exhibitions are taking place, and where to apply to book space. There may be several suitable ones each year.

Exhibitions can be expensive; as well as hiring the stand, you must arrange for someone competent to be there to man it, explain and perhaps demonstrate your product, distribute literature and note down enquiries (to be scrupulously followed up). Probably that person will have to be you, with consequent loss of your valuable time. The exhibition should at least earn back its expenses eventually, so do not rush in too readily without thought and preparation.

You are more likely to attract the buyers' attention if you write to them beforehand, preferably by name (which you can find out by telephoning their firms). Send them your promotional literature and the number of your stand, and invite them to have a chat with you.

If you cannot afford a stand, or if your range of goods does not rate one, ask the Chamber of Commerce or your Small Business Club for the names of any other firms who might be willing to share a stand. Or you may be able to find out from the promoters of the exhibition the names of firms who are exhibiting related products; approach them to ask if they will lease you a share of their space and attendants.

If you sell to a wholesaler and he is exhibiting, he will probably show your product, anyway, and will only need a supply of promotional literature; or you may be able to organise a joint venture with one of your suppliers.

direct mail advertising

With direct mail advertising, you approach the customer directly, and by name. You send out a sales letter, accompanied by a leaflet, brochure or catalogue. The promotional literature should be eye-catching, designed by a professional, if possible. There are special rates for first-time direct mail advertisers.

making the most of the post

Business reply and *Freepost* are two of the services offered by the Royal Mail to direct mail advertisers. With *Business reply*, you send out, for your customer's reply, a postcard or envelope printed with your address and needing no stamp: first and second class options are available. With *Freepost*, the customer can use either pre-printed cards or envelopes provided by you (first or second class), or use his own stationery (second class only). No stamp is needed if the word 'Freepost' is added to the address.

The charge is a 0.5p per item on top of ordinary first or second class postage, and you have to pay a licence fee (at present £20 per annum). But the Royal Mail offers special terms to first-time users of the reply-paid services, under which the first year's licence fee is waived, as are all charges on the first 500 replies delivered in that year.

A prepayment is required, equivalent to an estimated one month's charges. If this proves an under- or over-estimate, the charges for the following months are adjusted accordingly.

If you want to direct your advertising to one or more whole areas, rather than to specific addresses, you should find the *Household delivery service* useful. This arranges for your advertising to be delivered by the regular postmen on their rounds. The charge for this to you is based on the weight of the material: there are two weight categories, with a 60g maximum.

The minimum charge per 1000 items is £39.50 for the lower weight category, and £44 for the higher: this is for up to 10,000 items. There is a minimum charge of £100 per distribution. The more you send, the lower the rates, but it is unlikely that the most favourable rate, which assumes a distribution of more than ten million items, will be of interest to you in the early stages.

From October 1987 the Royal Mail is introducing Mailsort, a new range of discount services for presorted mail: these apply to bulk mailings of 4,000 or more items, provided these have been sorted in advance by the sender, according to postcode. Bear in mind, however, that you will have to pay someone to do the sorting, so these services are unlikely to prove useful to you until your business has expanded greatly.

Further details of these and other services can be obtained from the local postal services representative. You can find his number in the telephone directory, or write to Royal Mail Letters, ▲ Freepost, Room 195, 33 Grosvenor Place, London SW1X 1EE.

mailing lists

You do not, of course, write to the population at large; you need a mailing list of people likely to be interested.

If you want to sell to an industry or trade, you can make up your own mailing list out of entries in the trade directories; this is laborious but relatively inexpensive.

It is more effective if you can find out the name of each firm's buyer – from a trade reference book, the appropriate trade association or by telephoning the firm – and address the letter individually to him, making it appear unique. This is easy if you can get your letters prepared by a word processor (perhaps through a word processor bureau).

For advertising to local firms, relevant names and addresses from the Yellow Pages can be used in the same way.

For advertising to individual consumers, you can try to make up your own mailing list from the electoral register.

Many organisations have subscription or membership lists that they may be willing to rent out to you, for a fee. If the list is very large, they may agree to let you have part of it, or even just a very small part, so that you can test how well the list works for your purposes. Do not be too surprised, however, if the part that you are offered for the test turns out to be the best part of the list. To get a fairer idea of how useful the list is going to be to you, ask for a cross-selection – say, one out of every six names. A large percentage of any full list is likely to be postally undeliverable – 'no such address' or 'gone away'.

You may be able to buy the list, in which case you will receive the names and addresses and can use them as often as you like, for whatever purpose you like. However, very few organisations sell their lists; they rather rent them out or exchange lists. Exchanging means that two organisations use each others' lists – but you, as a beginner, will not have anything to swop.

The organisation may make it a condition to have sight of and approve the offer which is to be mailed. To prevent you from copying their lists, they may insist that the addressing and posting are done by a specialist mailing company.

You will, of course, learn the names and addresses of those who reply, and they then become part of your own list, which you later may sell, rent out or exchange. There are a number of list brokers who may be able to help you find lists, for a fee.

counting the cost

First calculate the likely cost, and be clear how to assess the responses. 25p per name and address may not sound much, but if the response rate is one per cent, the cost becomes £25 per reply.

The response rate to direct mail advertising is variable, depending on the product, the market and the care taken in preparation: a response of between 3 and 5 per cent should be considered as extremely good. Naturally, not every enquiry results in an order;

after your first mail shot you should be able to calculate whether the resulting business has earned back its promotion costs plus some profit.

Leaflet distribution is a humbler, localised version of direct mail. At its simplest, this could be a leaflet pushed through a few hundred neighbourhood doors by hired teenagers or an active retired person. You may be able to arrange for the newsagent to slip a leaflet inside every newspaper delivered, for a fee.

If you want to cover larger or more distant areas, you would have to entrust the work to a specialist firm: look in the Yellow Pages under Addressing/Circularising Services, and Circular/ Sample Distributors.

Two booklets called *The Small Businessman's Guide to Advertising* and *The Small Businessman's Guide to the Media* give useful advice on planning advertising campaigns on a modest scale: they are free from Thomson Local Directories, Thomson House, 296 Farnborough Road, Farnborough, Hants GU14 7NU (telephone: 0252-516111).

mailing preference service
The use of direct mail is a very effective form of advertising, but it needs to be used with particular care. Many members of the public resent receiving mail addressed to them by name, from a company with whom they have had no contact, and of whom they may not have heard: they are then very likely simply to throw away what they consider to be 'junk mail', without a second glance. It is therefore in the advertiser's interest to subscribe to the Mailing Preference Service (1 New Burlington Street, London W1X 5FD (telephone: 01-734 0058). The MPS makes available to the companies which subscribe to it, a quarterly listing of people who have positively requested that they should not be sent any direct mail advertising. It also makes available a list of those people who have asked to be sent more details of goods available in some particular category. If you do your mailing through a list broker or a mailing house, make sure that they use an 'MPS-cleaned' list.

press releases

Any event of special interest in your firm – the opening of a new workshop or the launching of a new product – should be communicated to the local and trade press, in the form of a press release. Do not be intimidated by 'press release' – all you have to do is find out who is in charge of the, say, technical page of the newspaper and then write to them with a suitable small article. Make sure that the relevant details are there of the product and of yourself, your name, your address, the prices. The better and more straightforwardly it is written, the more likely it is to get in. Pictures help, but they should be black and white. If what you send catches editorial attention, and secures a paragraph or two of editorial copy, this is often more effective than any advertisement. If you place an advertisement at the same time, you may get editorial mention – but the two are not invariably linked.

To get mentioned in the national press is helpful for anyone selling by mail order. Try to think who would be interested in your story, such as the women's page editor, perhaps.

selling

You will need to consider the question of distribution and selling long before you can manufacture enough to satisfy widespread demand.

selling to shops

At the most basic level, this is a question of taking round a sample of your product to appropriate shops in the district and persuading them to stock it. To go about this sensibly,

○ make an appointment to see the shop's owner or manager; do not simply turn up unannounced at the busiest time

○ make yourself familiar with competing products, their prices and their drawbacks, so that you can point out the advantages of yours (without obvious knocking)

○ be clear about the price of your product, but be willing to allow the retailer an attractive discount. The real problem is to decide whether to sell on sale or return, or not. On the whole, it is better not to, but if you find that one particular line does not move and others do, you could offer to buy it back in order to get the shop to take more of the stuff that does sell

○ be prepared to prove that you can guarantee supplies and will stick to delivery dates

○ have the product or range of your products properly packaged, as it will look when displaced in a shop window or shelf

○ sometimes it also helps to offer a small display aid, to show your product to its best advantage. Make clear to the shop owner that this is on loan to display your product, not a gift, nor for use to show off someone else's goods.

The technique for larger shops, or chain stores, is to start by contacting the appropriate buyer in each store. The retail directory (from a reference library) gives some names; find out others by telephoning. Make an appointment to see each buyer.

○ Pay particular attention to the presentation of your product.
○ Know your maximum capacity and the size of orders you can guarantee to deliver and your most dependable delivery dates.

○ Be prepared to prove that you can finance your increased output.
○ When you come to discuss the price, be sure to have some room for negotiating. But remember, some large shops will expect extended credit terms and will delay payment.

Most large companies pay on a 30-day account: that is, they pay invoices on their first accounting day occurring when 30 days have passed from receipt of the invoice. (That is why it is important to invoice customers promptly and correctly, offering no excuse for delaying payment.)

If you negotiate a major contract, ask for stage payments: for instance, part payment with the order and then percentage payments at various stages of production or delivery.

pricing

The price you charge for a product or service can be arrived at in various ways. Economists have theories about price based on cost, based on competition, based on the demand, based on the going rate; in real life for the small businessman, these categories tend to slide into each other.

Pricing based on costs is a crude but still commonly used method. The price is made up of the cost of the product to the manufacturer (labour, materials, overheads) plus a percentage mark-up to give what you consider to be a fair profit. Your own costs will set the lower limit.

This method, however, ignores two important factors: demand and competition. Unless you are selling bread during a famine, demand will set an upper limit on what you can charge, and so will the presence in the market of competitors.

You must allow for discounts for quantity orders, or for payment in seven days and for anything else that might encourage greater purchase or quicker settlement.

If you sell to the final consumer, by retail or through mail order, there is no problem with getting payment; but if you sell to another firm, you will need to offer credit – because the competition does – and you must cost that in.

If you sell through a wholesaler, your price must allow for the wholesaler's and retailer's profit as well as your own. The price to the customer will contain the three elements of the wholesaler's mark-up, the retailer's mark-up and your profit (plus VAT if applicable). You must allow for these in order not to price yourself out of the market.

pricing based on competition

It is important to identify your competitors and to make yourself familiar with what they are offering at what prices. You can, to a large extent, be guided by what competitors are asking for a comparable product.

For most products there are several price ranges, and manufacturers deliberately tailor their goods to fit into one of these. Some manufacturers produce several product ranges, each one for a different category. Cosmetics, for instance, tend to be cheap and cheerful for the young, medium priced for the average user, and extremely expensive for the richer consumer. You should decide at an early stage into which price category you product will slot.

If you cannot fit into the lower or middle range, because your costs are irreducibly high, you will have to aim at the higher category; but then you will have to make sure that the prices reflect some special and unique quality of your goods, and show the customer that this is so. There are some categories of goods – cosmetics, again, are an example – where a high price can actually be a selling point: the customer is reassured by it that she is getting a unique, luxury article, and it would be an error of psychology to charge less.

Another way of taking demand into account is this. If you produce a range of related goods, some will be more in demand than others: your pricing should therefore be based on a profit margin averaged out over the whole range.

Or you may try loss-leader pricing of one or more items, at cost, or very little above it, as a bait to capture a large share of the market quickly. But you will be the baiter bit if you sell all the low-profit items and none of the high-profit ones.

Pricing based on the going rate incorporates the elements of competition and of demand. It is the way of pricing in most service industries. Where there is no going rate, you must cost your own time very carefully when calculating your overheads. But, usually, there is a recognised going rate for the service, and in order to charge more, you would need to offer something out of the ordinary: such as being on call at all hours, or having unusually high qualifications, or offering a particularly comprehensive service.

face-to-face selling

Many people who would find no difficulty in selling goods across a shop counter, feel deeply embarrassed when it comes to calling on firms to offer their goods or services.

Aggressive selling is, however, rarely required: one's best weapon is a detailed knowledge of one's project and a readiness to explain it fluently, even demonstrate it.

Present as good an appearance as possible: as a small entrepreneur, you will inspire more confidence by a show of frugal efficiency than by lavish trimmings. (For some kinds of service only, such as consultancy perhaps, appearances are important, since you may have nothing else to show your client.)

Keep good records of your customers, how much they buy and when – a computer could prove useful there. Keep in constant touch, so that when they think of buying, you are in the forefront of their minds. Ask them if they are satisfied, and treat complaints in a friendly spirit; look into the complaint and put right anything that needs rectifying.

Genuinely listen to what the potential customer says, and show an obvious interest in what he or she wants.

In many cases you must be able to offer a service, as well as a product: installation, spare parts and servicing. Make sure that you have the facilities for this, or next time the customer may go elsewhere. If you cannot provide the service yourself, find a sub-contractor.

Know your potential customer's own products and be able to discuss them intelligently, and if you yourself happen to use his competitor's product, keep this to yourself.

employing an agent
If you dislike or have no talent for selling, or do not have time for it, you may be better occupied concentrating on the production side, while getting someone else to sell for you. You might think of persuading a golden-tongued friend to do you the favour, if only for the initial contacting, but a proper business partner, or, best of all for this purpose, a proper agent, is preferable.

The advantages for a new business can be considerable. An agent will have the necessary contacts, and be known in the trade; he can also keep you informed about what your competitors are doing. He will need to be primed with any necessary technical information and supplied with promotional literature, possibly backed with advertising.

The disadvantage is that the agent's commission reduces your profit margin – but perhaps you would not have had the profit at all, but for him.

An agent usually represents more than one firm, and you can never be sure that he is trying as hard for you as for the others: he naturally works hardest for products offering the highest return.

To find an agent, consult one or all of these: the trade press; trade directories; Yellow Pages (under Manufacturers' Agents and Marketing Consultants); or advertise for one yourself. You can negotiate any agreement that seems suitable, but both the agent and you must be quite clear about the terms before he starts.

mail order selling

Direct response mail order selling is a system in which press advertisements urge customers to order goods, which are then sent to them directly.

Payment is usually by cash (cheque) with order or by credit card; it is usual to offer free approval ('money back if not delighted') which is required by most of the relevant codes of practice; some firms offer credit terms, but these are usually catalogue mail order houses rather than firms selling their own products.

To be suitable for mail order selling, the product should fall into one or more of these categories:

○ Light in weight and strong enough not to break in transit, *or* bulky, but capable of being compactly and securely packed (for example, many types of garden sheds and greenhouses are sold by mail order)

○ Not obtainable in ordinary retail shops, that is, in some way new, unique or hard to find – for example a craft product, or something for a minority taste, *or*

obtainable in shops, but at a much higher price. Make sure, however, that the customer's postage costs do not take away your price advantage. Because of postage, very low-priced articles are not worth selling by mail.

Your customers must be left in no doubt about the total cost of any goods offered. In particular, make clear whether the costs of packing and postage or delivery are included in the price, and if not, what these costs are.

Not only your production but your packing, despatch and administration must be up to scratch. Before starting the operation, be sure that you have the stocks and the extra capacity to meet a sudden increase in demand, and are able to deliver goods within the promised period. This should be within 28 days.

If you suddenly find that an order cannot be sent off within the period you promised, you should immediately contact the buyer and offer a refund; or if the customer chooses to wait, he should be given a firm date for the despatch of the order.

These points, and very many others with which you must comply in this form of selling, are contained in the code of practice of the British Direct Marketing Association Ltd., 1 New Oxford Street, London WC1A 1NQ (telephone: 01-242 2254). The BDMA code is binding only on members of the Association. It follows, and reproduces much of, the British Code of Advertising Practice which is administered by the Advertising Standards Authority alongside the British Code of Sales Promotion Practice. Both codes can be obtained free of charge from the ASA.

You must conform to both the legal requirements and the voluntary codes of practice governing mail order selling. And to advertise in the national press, you must get clearance from the National Newspapers' Mail Order Protection Scheme Ltd., which runs a Mail Order Protection Scheme (MOPS) jointly with the

Incorporated Society of British Advertisers and the Institute of Practitioners in Advertising. You must pay an annual fee to a central fund which idemnifies readers against loss due to a firm's failure to supply goods ordered: you may, if you wish, display the MOPS logo in your advertisement.

Similar schemes are operated by many local papers and magazines. Advertising in the classified columns is exempt from the MOPS stipulations but you still have to get your advertising copy cleared. It must, in any event, conform to the British Code of Advertising Practice. To ensure that your advertisement will be acceptable, contact the Advertising Standards Authority: its Code of Advertising Practice secretariat will give you (free) advice and discuss your proposals with you.

The ASA's address is Brook House, 2–16 Torrington Place, ▲ London WC1E 7HN (telephone: 01-580 5555), and that of the National Newspaper Mail Order Protection Scheme is 16 Tooks ▲ Court, London EC4A 1LB (telephone: 01-405 6806).

Make sure that you have an efficient system (perhaps on computer) for recording the product sold, the dates of purchase and despatch, and the name and address of each customer (which is then added to your own mailing list – unless you subscribe to the mailing preference service and the customer's name is on the MPS 'removal' list). Note, however, that, if you process personal data of this type, you must register uses, sources and disclosures with the Data Protection Registrar and comply with the Code of Practice Covering the Use of Personal Data for Advertising and Direct Marketing Purposes – this is available from the Advertising Association, Abford House, 15 ▲ Wilton Road, London SW1V 1NJ (telephone: 01-828 2771). It is a criminal offence to collect or use personal data without having registered.

As with direct mail advertising, ask the postal services representative about reduced terms for bulk parcel despatch.

If you advertise in several newspapers and magazines, it is worth using a simple code to distinguish replies from each source, so that you can tell which one brings in the most business.

The price you charge for your product must take into account the advertising costs – often as much as $\frac{1}{3}$ of the selling price – as well as the cost of replacing damaged articles, and, if you offer credit, of bad debts. If you sell on credit, or free approval, allow for this in your cash flow forecasting.

Providing credit card facilities may be worth while, since it allows the customer to obtain credit without risk to yourself – your money is guaranteed, provided you adhere to the conditions.

To become a credit card agent, you have to approach the credit card area sales office (address from the head office or your local telephone directory). Within about ten days a representative will call to discuss the arrangements. There is a service charge or commission of up to 5 per cent plus, in most cases, a joining fee of £40 to £50.

Because in mail order selling there is no customer's signature on the credit card slip, you have to enter the details (customer's card number and its expiry date, the name and address, amount charged) and send this schedule to the headquarters of the card company. Goods over a certain value must not be despatched without written or telephone authorisation. Your account will be credited with the amount, minus the service charge or commission.

selling in a very small way
Market stalls and country fairs provide an outlet for a small business making a slow, cautious start at selling, and are particularly suited to craft goods. The local authority who do the licensing of stalls will be able to tell you where and when fairs are held in the district, and how to rent a stall, either permanently or by the day.

Exhibiting at a local craft fair could be a good way of launching a product. Some craft associations will arrange to exhibit members' work: you can find their addresses in the annual *Craftsman's Directory*, Brook House, Mint Street, Godalming, Surrey GU7 1HE (telephone: 048-68 22184). The *Showman's Directory* (same publisher) will give you a list of non-craft events throughout the country, which might be of use in finding appropriate locations for selling or publicity; it will also tell you where to hire marquees and other equipment.

PREMISES

The question of premises obviously varies according to the type of business. The kind of space you need to work in will depend largely on whether you manufacture goods, or sell them, or offer a service.

Offices, shops, factories and many other types of commercial accommodation have to comply with regulations about the safety of staff and facilities for them; so it is as well to be sure that one's prospective premises either accord with the regulations, or are capable of being converted so as to comply with them. Information about this can be obtained from the Health and Safety ▲ Executive, Baynards House, 1 Chepstow Place, London W2 4TF (telephone: 01-221 0870), or from the planning department of your local authority.

premises for a service industry

If you provide a service, for example as a builder, decorator, plumber, probably all of your work will be carried on in your customers' premises. To begin with, you will only need some space at home in which to do the paperwork, and perhaps a shed or garage for storing tools. However, if your business thrives and grows, and you come to employ workmen, you will eventually need an office to deal with enquiries, estimates and paperwork, and also larger storage space, and parking for your vans – proper business premises, in fact.

If your business is a consultancy or agency needing little or no equipment, you may require only a room or two, and may find it convenient to make over some part of your house to business use, or you may choose to rent a small office somewhere else. The physical location of your office may not be crucial to your success.

Obviously, for a very small and new business there is a tremendous advantage in working from home: you save on rent, rates, cost of the public utilities, cleaning – and even staff, if a member of your family answers the door and the telephone and perhaps does the typing.

However, some house deeds prohibit use for business purposes, and many restrictive covenants of this type would be
enforceable. Even where there are no such restrictions, if you
carry on a business from residential premises, you may need
planning permission from the local authority, and may have to
pay higher rates for commercial occupation. You should, in any
event, inform the company who is insuring your house. Using it
for business, particularly if you are storing any combustible
goods, many invalidate the buildings and contents insurance –
even against totally unrelated disasters, such as a burst water
pipe.

There are plenty of small businessmen who work inconspicu-
ously from home without permission and get away with it,
because there is nothing in their work to inconvenience the
neighbours or to alert snoopers. But if you want to be above-board
in carrying on your business, or if your house needs to be altered
in any way for the purpose, as in adding a room or shed, you may
need planning permission. There is a fee payable when an
application for planning permission is submitted to the local
authority.

Remember the potential capital gains tax liability on the portion
of your home used for business, when you come to sell the house.

The permission may be qualified by some conditions relating to
hours of work, or callers at the house. If your application is
refused, you have the right to appeal, but if this fails, you may
have no choice but to look for outside accommodation.

premises for a manufacturing business

Unless you are a craftsman working single-handed and in a very
small way of business, it is unlikely that you will be able to work
from home: apart from probable lack of workshop space, you will
run into opposition from the local authority.

A manufacturing firm has to satisfy zoning regulations for light
and heavy industry, because it may create noise, smoke, fumes,
industrial waste that must be disposed of, other sorts of environ-
mental pollution; or it may increase the risk of fire. It is extremely

unlikely that you could carry on a manufacturing business clandestinely, or that you would get permission to do so in residential premises.

As for renting workshop space, at the present time there are many millions of square feet of factory premises vacant in Britain, but only a small percentage of this is suitable for a business which is just starting up. Just the same, there is no reason why you should not get hold of some of this percentage if you go about it the right way.

hunting for workshop space
Define your exact requirements. You will need a site big enough to allow your firm to settle down and expand, because you may not want to have to move in a year or two. There must be access to all the mains services; warehousing space; room and amenities for the work-people; parking space; room for lorries to load and unload. You probably do not need a central situation or a street frontage, but you must ensure that any noise, fumes, smoke, do not annoy people living nearby, especially during overtime working.

You may need an office, if you expect customers to be calling on you. There may be a number of other requirements: it is unlikely that any one site will satisfy all of them.

Begin by applying to the local authority. Some authorities try to cater for the very small business by building 'nursery' units, which are simply shells, sometimes only 500 square feet (about the size of a double garage). The cost of building these is high, and so, consequently are the rents. But, if the authority is anxious to promote employment, it may offer you a short period rent-free.

The local authority may give you favourable rental terms, or even a rent-free period, if they want you out of a mainly residential area where your activities are unwelcome and you are what they call a 'non-conformer user', and the neighbours (can be persuaded to) campaign for your removal or closure.

Some councils keep a register of vacant industrial property, and may be able to help you by extracting from this a list of suitable properties. Most local authorities recognise that their attitude to small business can affect unemployment levels, and are as helpful as they can be.

But if official bodies cannot help, you must make the rounds of the estate agents. If you do resort to these, remember that they may need telephoning at intervals to remind them of your existence. Low-cost, low-rental premises have little value to an agent because they bring in a low fee. Very small and cheap premises in the centre of town do not always reach the estate agents' lists, so keep your own eyes open, and also study the classified advertisements in the local press.

When you find a place that seems suitable, there are still a number of factors to be considered, for instance, whether to buy or to lease. Most people starting a small business are likely to want to keep their capital readily available rather than sink it in buying property (and mortgage repayments can be a burden). So you would be well advised to rent premises in the first instance, on as short a lease as possible, and so minimise your responsibilities. However, you should be assured of having the option of renewing the lease, and for a longer period, otherwise you may have to move just when you least want to. You would have a statutory right to apply to the county court for a new lease, but the landlord may contest this. Moreover, since your original lease was short, the court may grant only a brief extension, not long enough to find other premises. Have your lease vetted by a solicitor experienced in such matters: do not try to do your own conveyancing.

It is unwise to rent or buy a building without having a survey done; you might have unpleasant surprises later, when structural or other faults may come to light. If the survey sounds expensive, talk to the surveyor about a negotiated fee. You do not want a lengthy catalogue listing features that you can see for yourself, nor a full unlimited guarantee on which you could sue if he missed anything. What you want is a realistic guide to the value of the property and what you must do to it soon, what you can risk leaving for a while, and what is unimportant structurally. Such information is as useful given orally as it would be in a typed document, and is far cheaper, especially if it is without the insurance-underwritten indemnity.

If the property is an older one which you will have to refurbish at your own expense, you will be increasing its value to the owner, so you may be able to negotiate a cheaper rent.

Check that there will be no difficulties with the mains services, that there will be enough electric power, water, gas, and also adequate drainage, and no difficulties about the telephone.

Somebody who is a low user of water should ask the water undertaking or water authority to be allowed to be metered instead of being charged a fixed rate.

fire prevention

Premises require a fire certificate if they are used as a place of work, a shop, factory or office where more than 20 people are employed, or more than 10 people elsewhere than on the ground floor; or if explosives or highly inflammable substances are stored there.

If you are moving into previously occupied premises, find out whether there is a current fire certificate, and if so, whether it covers your operations. If your occupancy constitutes a change of conditions because of structural alterations, a change of use, or change in the number of persons working, you will need a new certificate.

Your local fire prevention officer grants the certificate if he is satisfied, after inspecting the premises, that all necessary precautions have been taken.

Consult your fire prevention officer before you clinch the deal for any premises: if your work means installing a number of fire escapes, fire doors, new flooring, this may prove to be too expensive to be worth while. You cannot argue with a fire prevention officer: his word is law with no appeal, and he can close you down without notice. You may find that until you have satisfied the demands of fire prevention, you will be refused any other kind of permission that may also be required.

Even if you do not need a fire certificate, your premises must have adequate means of escape, and fire-fighting equipment.

planning permission

Make sure that the premises you choose already have the planning permission that you will need. Otherwise you will have to
apply to the local authority's planning department for permission
to make alterations or to change the use of the premises. Obtaining this can take months (and there are fees to be paid).

If you take the local authority's planners into your confidence
from the start, they may prove remarkably helpful, and eager not
to thwart a new business, unless there are overwhelming objections to the plans you put forward.

If you intend to start from a green field site and build on it,
planning permission will take much longer, and is only one of the
obstacles to be overcome.

rates and concessions

If you are not tied to any one area and can set up anywhere, you
may do best in an assisted area, where you may sometimes get
rent-free accommodation for up to two years, perhaps in a
purpose-built factory.

▲   English Estates, Methven House, Kingsway, Team Valley,
Gateshead, NE11 0LN (telephone: 091-487 4711) provide industrial
and commercial premises of all sizes in the assisted areas and
offer a range of services, including easy in-easy out terms and an
in-house business support service for all tenants.

Many local authorities are prepared to give initial rate relief to
new businesses, and those relocating themselves into the area.
Get in touch with the planning department or the economic unit
of your local authority about these or other concessions.

If you intend to set up businesses in a rural area, consult the
local CoSIRA office which may know of small properties, converted
barns, or other accommodation available for rent.

sublet premises

If you need only a modest amount of space, you may be able to
find an existing business which has spare capacity, and is glad to
reduce its overheads by subletting to you.

The kind of business to look for is one in a similar but not
competing line of business: the association could even result in a
partnership.

SQUARING UP TO ACCOUNTS

The figures that your business generates are an an index of its health and growth. Many people in a small business seem to be positively scared of them and keep no continuous control.

It is not good enough to monitor the state of health of the business by the annual accounts, which are not available until the following year is well advanced. If anything is then found to be amiss, it may well be too late to put it right.

You may feel that, if you employ an accountant, it is his business to keep an eye on the figures on the why-keep-a-dog-and-bark-yourself? principle. But an accountant should rather be thought of as a doctor: he cannot compel you to look after your business health properly, he can only diagnose the sickness resulting from your imprudence, and he certainly cannot cure it once it has become terminal.

So, do not be scared of your accounts and take an informed interest in what the figures show you.

You should know at the end of each month, if not every week, whether it has been a profitable one, and whether you have enough money in hand or on tap, to cover your expenses for the coming month. Your calculations need not be very elaborate: quite rough monthly accounts, backed up by an accountant's quarterly report, will enable you to stay in control.

what you can do for yourself
Your accountant could, of course, carry out your monthly monitoring for you; but it is most unlikely that your new, small business could afford the expense. If you do this work for yourself, you will be in a position to know, at all times, what is happening to your business, and to forecast what is going to happen next.

What is more, you will then have no trouble in understanding the accountant's quarterly reports, and relating them to your own day-to-day experience. Even if you prefer to have your account-ant do all the figure work, you must be able to make sense of the reports he prepares for you.

keeping business records

There are excellent reasons why you should keep good business records: because the Inland Revenue and Customs and Excise (for VAT) require it, because your bank manager may require regular information, and because you will save your accountant's time (which he charges for by the hour). But the most important reason is that properly kept accounts, summarised at the end of each month and coupled with a stocktake or an estimate of the value of your stock, will give you the up-to-date knowledge of your affairs which you need to spot danger signs while there is still time to put things right and to plan ahead for further improvements or expansion, if things go well.

who keeps the books?
Although all modern double-entry book-keeping follows the same general pattern, no two firms' sets of books are identical: every business has some individual aspects which must be recorded, and every businessman has his own notions of which of these records he needs to monitor.

So get your accountant, who understands your particular requirements, to set up your books for you, and to teach you how to keep them. He will probably do so willingly, for it is to his advantage, as well as yours, to be presented with clear, well-kept books to deal with. Or, better still, ask him to teach some member of your family whom you can conscript to relieve you of the task. It is not difficult, and it will probably be some time before your business demands the services of a fulltime trained book-keeper.

You can also teach yourself the elements of book-keeping from one of a variety of books on the subject, but be sure to acquire this skill before you start up, because you will not have time afterwards.

the records you must keep
Business records may be kept and presented in a variety of ways, and depend very much on the type of business for their format.

However, one feature is common to all systems: they must be

backed by evidence that the receipts and payments recorded have actually been made. So be sure to keep safely all of the following:

○ cheque-book stubs
○ cancelled cheques (tell the bank to return them to you)
○ bank paying-in books (use them, not paying-in slips)
○ bank statements (make sure that you have separate accounts – even if they are at the same bank – for business and private life, whether you are sole trader or partnership or company)
○ copies of your own invoices, receipts and delivery notes
○ your suppliers' invoices, receipts and delivery notes
○ receipts, wherever possible, for minor expenditure made in cash.

the books
For keeping accounts, even at their simplest, you must keep several books.

The cash book is the most basic account book: it records all your payments and receipts made by cheque (for this purpose cheques are regarded as cash) or in ready money.

Some businesses are purely cash ones – that means that, whether you are buying or selling, payment is made immediately. If yours is not one of these, and you buy and sell with payment at a later date, you will need two further books, a sales day book for recording your sales invoices as they are sent out, and a purchases day book in which are recorded your purchases of goods and services.

This last book, which is all-important, will be of the kind called an analysis book, ruled with a number of vertical columns, in which you classify your different kinds of expenditure: materials, direct labour and the various sorts of overheads. Be sure to get a book with enough columns; how many you will need depends on your particular expenses, and on how minutely you want to break them down.

By adding up each column every month, you will see exactly how much each of your business expenses came to. The total of these totals will give you your whole month's costs.

If you are registered for VAT, you will have a VAT column in both your sales and your purchases books, to record the amount of VAT that other people pay you, and that which you pay; this information you will need for your quarterly VAT return.

If you employ anyone, you must keep a record of wages paid, showing gross earnings, deductions for income tax, National Insurance, any pension scheme, any other deductions, net pay and the employer's National Insurance contributions. You can obtain a proprietary wages book system from a business stationer. If you decide to use a micro-computer in your business, you can buy a program that will attend to the wages records for you.

The petty cash book is a record of small out-of-pocket expenses paid by you or your staff in the course of work. It may include any number of different things, such as fares, taxis, the window-cleaner and the tea bought for tea-breaks. The money is paid out of a float drawn at intervals from the bank (and duly recorded in the cash and purchase books). The petty cash book is on the same lines as the purchases book, with columns for different sorts of expenditure.

slightly more advanced book-keeping

As your business expands and becomes more complex, you will need to start keeping ledgers.

The sales ledger is based on the sales day book, and records the individual accounts of each of your customers, showing how much he has bought in any given period and the date of his payments. This enables you to keep an eye on slow payers. (It is also invaluable in planning future marketing strategy. It may show, for instance, that 80 per cent of your trade is with a few customers placing substantial orders, and 20 per cent is with a large number of small customers. You will then have to decide whether to go on accepting small orders whose costs are high in relation to the profits, in the hope that the small customers may be encouraged to grow into bigger ones.)

The purchases ledger is based on the purchases day book, and records your transactions with each of your suppliers. It shows which of them are getting the largest share of your custom; these will be the ones most likely to give credit or offer generous cash discounts.

The general ledger records impersonal payments, that is the sale and purchase of equipment, rent and rates, services, etc, and the totals of income and expenditure.

These ledgers are the foundation for a double entry book-keeping system. A full explanation of this would require a book to itself, but the principle on which it is based is a simple one: it is that every transaction must be recorded twice, once as a debit and once as a credit, according to whether it is regarded from a buyer's or a seller's point of view.

Every sale you make represents a debit entry to your customer in the sales ledger and a credit to you in the sales account in the general ledger: when the customer pays, this appears as a debit entry in the cash book and a credit entry in the sales ledger.

Every purchase you make from your supplier is a credit entry for him in your purchases ledger and a debit for you in the general ledger. When you pay up, this is recorded as a credit in your cash book and a debit for the supplier in the purchases ledger.

using what your figures tell you

With all these records, you are in a position to make calculations showing how your business is progressing. The all-important one is your monthly net profit. To arrive at this, you need to draw up a monthly trading account and a profit and loss account. The monthly trading account shows the gross profits of your business. You calculate it by adding together your month's labour and materials costs, and the difference between the value of your opening and closing stocks, and subtracting this from the total monthly sales figure.

Jack's product sells at £20 per unit; of this, his materials cost £10, and labour costs £2. His overheads are £800 a month. Using the sales, purchase and labour totals shown by his books, Jack draws up a trading account, thus:

JACK'S TRADING ACCOUNT FOR ONE MONTH

	£			£
Opening stock			Sales	4,000
(100 units @ £12)	1,200			
Purchases of materials				
(200 @ £10)	2,000			
Labour (200 @ £2)	400			
	3,600			
Less closing stock				
(80 @ £12)	960			
	2,640			
Balance, i.e. gross				
profit	1,360			
	4,000			4,000

Jack has valued his stock at materials and labour costs only:
overheads do not enter the calculation until the next step, the
monthly estimated net profit. This is how it looks in Jack's case:

JACK'S PROFIT AND LOSS ACCOUNT

	£			£
Overheads	800		Gross	
			profit	1,360
Balance, i.e.				
net profit	560			
	1,360			1,360

This is the most basic way of drawing up a profit and loss account.
It can, in fact, be combined with the trading account in a single
calculation. There is no special presentation that must be followed.

You can make it more informative by making it more complex:
you can isolate and thus spotlight items of overheads or other
factors that you particularly want to keep an eye on, for instance,
the cost of power consumption. Or, because power is a cost that

varies with the volume of production, you could choose to treat it as a materials purchase, rather than an overhead.

Here we have assumed that Jack's enterprise is a limited company and his salary is therefore one of the overheads. If he were a sole trader, his remuneration (say, £350 a month) would not be included in the overheads, which would then be £450 a month, and the month's net profit before tax would be £910, and would constitute Jack's taxable income.

However, you may have a profit and loss account that looks as healthy as this one, and still run out of funds, because it does not show that at any one time you may not actually have in hand all the money due to you. If your suppliers demand cash on delivery while your customers will only place orders on 30 or 60 day credit terms, and your expanding business is demanding additional unforeseen expenditure, you have got a cash flow problem.

cash flow forecasting
The drawing up of a cash flow forecast has already been explained. In the examples that follow, the tables are considerably simplified; in particular, they ignore VAT and assume equal monthly overheads.

Jack's latest cash flow forecast looks like this (figures in brackets denote a deficit):

Month	Jan.	Feb.	Mar.	Apr.	May
	£	£	£	£	£
Opening bank balance/(overdraft)	(3,000)	(2,200)	(1,400)	(600)	200
Payments:					
purchases	2,000	2,000	2,000	2,000	2,000
labour	400	400	400	400	400
overheads	800	800	800	800	800
Maximum borrowing requirement	6,200	5,400	4,600	3,800	3,000
Receipts from sales	4,000	4,000	4,000	4,000	4,000
Closing balance/(overdraft)	(2,200)	(1,400)	(600)	200	1,000

Jack has now been asked to take on a regular order for another 200 units a month, but with payment only after 90 days. This means another machine at £500, plus additional part-time labour costs, and it will take two months to build up the manufacturing capacity. In order to be in a position to decide whether to accept the order, Jack prepares another forecast, which looks like this:

CASH FLOW FORECAST II
(figures in brackets denote a deficit)

Month	Jun.	July	Aug.	Sept.	Oct.	Nov.	Dec.
Products made	200	300	400	400	400	400	400
	£	£	£	£	£	£	£
Opening balance/ (overdraft)	1,000	300	(1,300)	(2,900)	(4,500)	(4,100)	(1,700)
Payment:							
purchases	3,000	4,000	4,000	4,000	4,000	4,000	4,000
labour	400	800	800	800	800	800	800
overheads	800	800	800	800	800	800	800
Capital expenditure	500						
Maximum borrowing requirement	3,700	5,300	6,900	8,500	10,100	9,700	7,300
Receipts from sales	4,000	4,000	4,000	4,000	6,000	8,000	8,000
Closing balance/ (overdraft)	300	(1,300)	(2,900)	(4,500)	(4,100)	(1,700)	700

It shows him that if he accepts the order under these conditions, he will be overdrawn for five months, and will need a further investment of around £4,500 for 3 months, to pay for the additional costs. The bank might well be willing, on the basis of this profitable order, to lend the money to a customer who had already succeeded in repaying an overdraft of £3,000. To minimise his borrowing requirement, Jack might be able to persuade his suppliers to agree to a delayed payment, and might also be able to dovetail this payment into those months when no major overheads were due.

In order to keep the example simple, two other factors have been excluded: the cost of additional power consumption resulting from increased production, and the interest payable on bank loans or overdrafts; but a rough calculation is all that is wanted at this stage.

Jack's experience shows that for a small, newly-established firm, a large order, unaccompanied by prompt payment, can be a disaster if there is no means of stretching resources to cover the expenditure demanded by the additional output. By making a forecast on similar lines, you will be able to see how your money supply will relate to your expenditure.

Having discovered what your volume of production is to be in the next six months, or so, your next task is to discover at which point you will begin to make a profit.

break-even point

Every business has a break-even point, at which it is producing just enough for the receipts to balance the costs. Before this point is reached, it is working at a loss; when it is passed, the business is showing a profit.

In a manufacturing business, the break-even point is measured in units of production; in a service one, in the number of paid hours worked.

fixed and variable costs

The costs of manufacturing anything can be divided into two categories: fixed and variable.

Fixed costs are the ones which remain the same whatever the amount you manufacture: the overheads and, in the short term, labour.

Variable costs are those which vary with the amount you manufacture, such as materials and power.

Some costs are partly fixed and partly variable, for example, power, which you are bound to use to some extent even without manufacturing anything: they should be split, in calculations, into their fixed and variable elements. However, in the example that follows, power has, for the sake of simplicity, been treated as an overhead.

In the case of George, another manufacturer, the relationship between his volume of production (number of units made and sold in a month) and his profitability is as follows:

Units made	Variable cost	Fixed cost	Total cost	Receipts from sales	Profit/ (loss)
20	200	1,200	1,400	400	(1,000)
60	600	1,200	1,800	1,200	(600)
100	1,000	1,200	2,200	2,000	(200)
140	1,400	1,200	2,600	2,800	200

These figures can be expressed in a graph. The horizontal axis represents the number of units produced, the vertical axis represents money: on this are plotted George's selling price and total cost at each volume of production. The two lines intersect at the point at which production is 120 units: this is where he is just covering his costs, and beyond this, he will begin to make a profit.

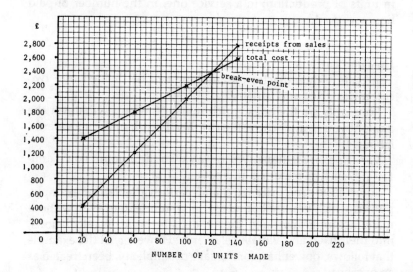

A calculation and simple graph like this will enable you to plan your volume of production intelligently in relation to your financial resources. You can use it to explore the way in which fixed costs, variable costs, sales prices and profits affect each other. For instance, you may wish to expand manufacture to an extent which will increase your fixed costs: can you maintain profits, bearing in mind your probable increase in variable costs?

Never forget to revise your cash flow forecast when you expect a change in circumstances, particularly if you are thinking of expanding production in search of higher sales.

balance sheet

At any time after starting up, you may want to analyse your deployment of your resources: the balance sheet constitutes such an analysis. You will need – and any substantial lender will require – not just a year-end balance sheet, but also intermediate ones, or the details for them at regular intervals. You can then observe what the trend is in any particular matter that you want to analyse.

A balance sheet shows the financial state of the firm at a given date and is based on the account balances in the ledgers at that date.

It takes account of what the business owns (its assets), and of what it owes (its liabilities). Both of these may be subdivided into fixed and current ones.

– *Fixed liabilities* are debts which are repayable over a long period of time.

– *Current liabilities* are those which must be repaid in the short term, such as debts to suppliers, overdrafts, and interest on loans.

– *Fixed assets* are property such as land, buildings, plant, machinery and vehicles. (These need to be revalued periodically, and their book value adjusted; land and buildings tend to increase in value with inflation, while plant, machinery and vehicles depreciate and have to be replaced. It is useful to set up a sinking fund or reserve for an eventual replacement cost.)

– *Current assets* include customers' book debts, the value of any stock held, and money in hand or in the bank.

– *Quick assets* are the narrow type of current assets represented by money; by assets which can be quickly converted to money, such as Stock Exchange securities; and by some short-term book debts, where these are by customers in good standing. Raw materials are not included nor, generally, are finished goods.

From the figures for assets and liabilities you can make several kinds of analysis. For example, you can look at the ability of your business to meet its commitments. Is it solvent? That is, would it be able to pay its outside creditors in full (if necessary by selling all its assets)?

It is easier to compare balance sheet positions if you convert the actual figures into a ratio or percentage of solvency.

Another test of solvency is to see whether the business, as a going concern, can meet its current liabilities out of its current assets; again, it is usual to express this in the form of a ratio. This 'current ratio' should usually be rather better than 1:1, because not all current assets may be easily saleable, so a margin of safety is prudent.

A further test – the acid test – is to see how far current liabilities can be paid out of quick assets; expressed as the 'quick ratio', this will be less than the current ratio, and often less than 1:1. In all these tests, you need to be sure that you are using up-to-date realistic sale values for the assets.

Your accountant will be able to advise you about choosing the ratios that are appropriate for your own particular business, and can also tell you about some other useful analyses that you can make.

In George's case, his resources have been as follows: £3,000 capital; an overdraft facility of £2,000, of which he is at present using only £1,200; a medium-term bank loan of £2,500 to buy plant and machinery. His profit has not been taken out, but kept in reserve to be used to buy additional plant and to provide additional working capital. The astute businessman would invest his reserves, if these were not needed immediately, which would then be entered as 'investments' on the asset side of the balance.

George's simplified balance sheet might look like this:

George's balance sheet at 1 January 1986

	£	£	£
ASSETS:			
Fixed assets:			
plant and machinery	6,500		
motor vehicles	4,000		
	10,500		
Less hire-purchase debt	2,000	8,500	
Current assets:			
stock	1,000		
debtors	2,500	3,500	12,000
LIABILITIES:			
Medium-term bank loan		2,500	
Current liabilities:			
Creditors	2,800		
overdraft	1,200	4,000	6,500
TOTAL NET ASSETS			5,500
Resources to generate these net assets are:			
George's capital introduced into business			3,000
George's undrawn profits left in business			2,500
			£5,500

Assuming that George has used realistic values for the assets, then, even in a forced sale, the business is solvent. But it cannot meet current liabilities out of current assets: there is a £500 shortfall (£4,000 as against £3,500). Even less can it meet current liabilities out of 'quick' assets: there is a £1,500 shortfall, so this balance sheet is weak. We know, however, that George has £800 unused overdraft facility, and he may possibly have extra personal funds, which he could introduce. But, on the face of it, the business depends on the continued renewal of overdraft arrangements, which makes it vulnerable.

This is only one balance sheet: a whole series of them might show that this single one gives an unusually poor impression of the business. One balance sheet a year cannot ever be informative enough.

There are many ways of presenting a balance sheet, and individual items can be more closely analysed; for instance, stock can be divided into finished stock and raw materials. If you are making your balance sheet, keep it simple to begin with; if an accountant does it for you, be sure that he does it in a form that you can understand.

The very basic balance sheet shown on p. 93 does not take account of the difference between a sole trader (or partnership) and a limited company. In actual practice, the balance sheet of a company would have to be drawn up rather differently. Its capital would have to be shown among the liabilities, because it belongs, not to the company, but to its shareholders. The same is true of the net profit on the trading account: it must ultimately be distributed among the shareholders. In a sole-trader firm or partnership, the capital investment and the profits are owned by the firm and are, therefore, assets.

factoring

If you are in real cash flow trouble, perhaps because you have reached your bank borrowing limit and have a lot of customers owing you money which they are in no hurry to pay, you could possibly resort to factoring. The factoring company advances you the money owing on your customers' invoices, and retains a percentage as commission when they are paid.

Consult your bank manager for the name of a suitable company. Most factoring companies are backed by clearing banks or other major financial organisations. One disadvantage is that they often take only those firms which have a turnover in excess of a set (very high) amount.

It is an expensive way of buying money and only to be resorted to if things are – temporarily – desperate, not as a standard way of bridging the gap between outgoings and receipts, or to ensure that slow paying customers do not lock up your working capital.

As a rule of trading, you should do all you can to induce those who owe you money to pay as quickly as possible, while paying your own bills with as much delay as possible. In both cases, the discount for quick payment is at stake; you must either give it to your customers or forfeit it from your suppliers. But in any event, a cash discount given or forfeited is likely to cost considerably less than the factoring commission.

TAXATION AND THE SMALL BUSINESS

When you set up in business for yourself, you come up against taxation in several different ways. You may pay:

o income tax on your individual earnings, or on your profits, if you are a sole trader or partnership
o corporation tax on your profits if yours is a limited company, and if you are in the happy situation of making some profits
o value added tax (VAT).

All taxes are liable to change at any time, not only with each year's budget. The monthly up-dating service of Croner's *Reference Book for the Self-employed and Smaller Business* (Croner House, 173 Kingston Road, New Malden, Surrey KT3 3SS, telephone: 01-942 8966) can be consulted at any time for the latest figures.

the first thing to do
As soon as you are ready to start trading, you should inform

o the inspector of taxes for your trading district
o your local Customs and Excise department (the VAT office), if there is any chance that you may want or need to be registered
o your local Department of Health and Social Security, about national insurance.

Look up the local offices in your telephone directory; among the useful explanatory publications which they will send you, on request, are: *Starting in business* issued by the Board of Inland Revenue (IR.28) which includes a list of relevant leaflets; one on *Corporation Tax* (IR.18), also issued by the Board of Inland Revenue; *The Value Added Tax guide* (notice 700) and leaflets entitled *Should I be registered for VAT?*; *The ins and outs of VAT*; *Filling in your VAT return* all isssued by HM Customs and Excise. *VAT Publications* (700/13A/85), lists these, and also leaflets dealing specifically with many individual types of business.

income tax: directors of companies
If yours is a limited company, you, as one of its full-time directors, are an employee: you therefore pay income tax on your salary and on any bonus under the PAYE system, like any other employee. At the start of each trading year, you determine what your annual salary is to be, and you pay it to yourself monthly or weekly. Each time, you deduct income tax, according to instructions provided by Inland Revenue, to whom you send the deducted amounts. (In practice, this may be done not every week or month but, with the Inland Revenue's agreement, once a year.)

If, at the end of the trading year, the company accounts show a profit, you have the option of taking some or all of this profit as additional salary or bonus, and deducting tax from it. If there is another director with more than a nominal holding, the additional money would, of course, be distributed in proportion.

Whatever part of the profits is not taken in salary, is liable for (or, in Inland Revenue jargon, 'charged to') corporation tax. It is for you, in consultation with your accountant, to decide whether it is to your advantage to pay more income tax or more corporation tax; no general ruling is possible.

income tax: sole traders and partnerships
If you are a sole trader, or a partnership, there is no decision to be made: the whole of your business profits are treated as sole trader's or partner's income and taxed accordingly (under Schedule D); corporation tax does not apply.

choosing your accounting year
A firm's accounts are made up annually. This does not apply to the first trading period, which may be shorter than a year, or, for a sole trader or partnership, longer. But it is usual to call the day of the year on which you first close your books, your annual accounting date, and to go on using this day as the end of the trading year for as long as the firm continues in business.

It is for you to decide which day is to be your year's end. You may make it coincide with the end of the tax (financial) year, i.e. April 5th; or with the end of the calendar year: or you may choose any other date at all. The Board of Inland Revenue suggests that if yours is a seasonal business, you should arrange to end your year in a slack period; your accountant may suggest a date soon after April 5th because, as will be explained later, this gives you the longest period for paying your taxes.

presenting accounts for inspection

The inspector of taxes requires to see the firm's trading account and profit and loss account, and sometimes the balance sheet (depending on the business concerned). He can ask for complete records of the whole of the firm's payments and receipts (including what has been drawn for private expenditure), supported by invoices, receipts, bank records and statements, paid cheques and cheque stubs.

It is best if the accounts are professionally drawn up by an accountant. Not only does he know the accepted way of presenting them, but he is able to make computations of allowances and adjustments which determine, after consultation with the tax inspector, what proportion of the profits is taxable. It is in your interest to make sure that all allowances are correctly claimed; this is a complex matter, best entrusted to an expert.

allowances on capital expenditure

Capital expenditure is money spent on plant, buildings, machinery, vehicles, and anything else that has an enduring benefit for the business and does not need to be renewed every year. It is not, in itself, tax deductible, but allowances may be given for the expenditure. In the case of a sole trader, these are set off against income for tax purposes. There used to be two different forms of tax allowance on capital expenditure: a 'first-year' or 'initial' allowance (sometimes up to 100 per cent of expenditure) and a smaller, annual 'writing down' allowance, which could be claimed either instead of the initial allowance, or, if this allowance was less than 100 per cent, to obtain the balance of the expenditure.

The initial allowance has now been phased out, except in some exceptional cases: for instance, in the case of a business in an enterprise zone. If you start up in one of these, you will still qualify for a 100 per cent first-year allowance on business buildings: there are no present plans to abolish this.

The annual writing down allowance can still generally be claimed, but you should check with the tax office that your intended expenditure qualifies. The benefit to you depends on the rate of allowance for the particular expenditure, the date on which it was incurred, and the timing of your claim. This can be a complicated business, and you will do well to consult your accountant when thinking of making a substantial capital purchase.

deductible expenses

A portion of those expenses which are incurred wholly in the course of conducting the business can be set off against tax. Some of these are:

- wages of wife employed in the business (but they must be included in the husband's tax return as wife's income)
- expenses of business travel (but not of going to and from home to the main place of work unless a business call is made en route)
- interest on business loans
- interest charges on hire-purchase of capital equipment
- hire or leasing of equipment
- insurance premiums
- bad debts
- entertainment for overseas customers
- subscriptions to trade and professional associations
- cost of self-employed retirement annuity.

If your house or telephone are used partly for your business, you may claim against tax a proportion of the expenses (rent, rates, telephone rental, light, heating and so on). But if you claim half the rates against tax and, for the period of your business only half the house is residential and the other half is commercial, when, later on, you sell the house, there will be a potential capital gains tax liability on the appreciation in value during that time: half the amount of the increase in value.

In the case of a car, some proportion of its cost (corresponding to the proportion of business use), may be claimed as capital allowance, and a similar proportion of the running costs may be claimed as a deductible business expense. You must, therefore, keep a record of the business mileage and the total mileage.

tax-deductible losses
Since a sole trader's (or partnership's) profits are taxed as income, losses may be set off against any income that the trader or his wife may receive from some other sources, in that year and the next.

Losses incurred in the first 4 years of trading may be set against wages or other income received in the 3 years before the trading loss was incurred: a part of all the tax paid during that period will be refunded.

These are useful and valuable options. The sole trader can also choose to carry the losses forward to future business years to set against future profits. He would need special reasons to choose to do that (and he would, of course, lose the other two options): one reason would be that in the past he had not had much income and therefore had paid little or no tax. Early trading losses would then be more useful if set against future profits.

how business income tax is assessed
As a general rule, the tax assessment of a sole trader or partnership is based on profits which were earned in the accounting year which ended in the previous tax year.

However, in the first 3 years of a new business, there are special rules for assessing business profits for tax. They are as follows:

First tax year (that is the year in which the business commenced): tax is assessed on profits from day 1 of trading up to April 5th: if the accounting year ends at some later date, a proportion is calculated on a time basis.

Second tax year: income tax is assessed on the profits of the first 12 months of trading; again, if the accounting year is different, apportionment applies.

Third tax year: income tax is assessed on the accounting year ending in the previous tax year.

An example will help to make this clear. Tom started trading on May 5th, 1980, fixing May 4th as his year's end (accounting date). In his first trading year, his taxable profits were £900; in his second, they were £1,800; in his third, £2,400; in his fourth, £3,000.

tax year (6th–5th April)	assessment period from	to	taxable profits £
1980–1981	5.5.80	5.4.81	825 (11/12 of 900)
1981–1982	5.5.80	4.5.81	900
1982–1983	5.5.80	4.5.81	900
1983–1984	5.5.81	4.5.82	1,800
1984–1985	5.5.82	4.5.83	2,400
1985–1986	5.5.83	4.5.84	3,000

This shows that a new business's profits in the first 3 years are assessed on the basis of the first 12 months of trading, when profits are likely to be at their lowest. As they begin to increase, the basis of assessment shifts, until, in its fourth year, the assessment period follows the general rule for established businesses. Generally speaking, therefore, the first 12 months' profits should be kept as low as possible for tax purposes because they are the basis for two or even three years' tax bills.

an optional basis of assessment
The trader has the choice of being assessed, in his second and third year of trading (both, not just one of these), on the actual profits made in those years, and not on the first trading period. Obviously, this option will be to his advantage only if his profits in the second and third years are lower than his first.

when tax is payable
Income tax is payable in two instalments, due on 1st January and 1st July. It is when you come to pay it that the importance of a good accounting date becomes apparent. Tom's trading period

ends one month after the end of the tax year, which means that he will not be assessed for tax till nearly a year after his annual accounts are made up, and will not have to pay the tax till the following January and July. In fact, by choosing the right accounting date, you can obtain more than 2 years' grace from Inland Revenue.

changes to sole traders and partnerships
If a sole trader decides to take a partner, or a partnership takes an additional partner (or partners) or loses one or more, then for income tax purposes the business is usually deemed to have stopped trading when the old arrangement ended, and to have started trading again when the new arrangement started.

However, this need not happen for tax purposes if all parties to both arrangements request the tax inspector, within 2 years of the change, to treat the trading as continuing.

corporation tax: limited companies
Most of what has been said about income tax on business profits (also known as Schedule D income tax) applies to the payment of corporation tax. Here are the main differences between the two.

Corporation tax is the tax which companies pay on their profits. There are two different rates for 1987–88: the full rate of 35 per cent, and the reduced 'small company rate' of 27 per cent.

A small company is currently defined as one whose annual profits are £100,000 or less: up to this amount, the lower tax rate of 29 per cent is charged on all profits. Above this, the rate of tax gradually increases, according to a complex formula, until at £500,000 the full rate of 35 per cent applies, on all profits.

Whatever rate of tax is charged, it applies not only to the excess over £100,000, but to the total amount of profit: profits over £100,000 hoist up the tax charged on amounts below this sum. Should you find yourself making profits of this order, you will need to ask your accountant how you can legitimately reduce your tax liability.

how not to pay corporation tax
One material difference between a sole trader and a company lies in the fact that the salaries paid to company directors are a business cost, like any other salaries, and so are deducted in calculating profits. As the directors' remuneration need not be fixed until the results of the year's trading are known, it may be advantageous to a small company to pay out all its trading surplus as directors' salaries, on which they pay individual income tax. (For the remuneration to qualify as a deduction, however, the company must be able to show that it was paid or was made available 'wholly and exclusively for the purpose of the trade'.) Any part of the surplus that is not paid out is known as 'retained profit' and taxed at the corporation tax rate.

Your accountant will advise you how to apportion your profits between salaries and retained profit to your best advantage. He will also be needed for drawing up the accounts because, although corporation tax returns are not particularly complicated, the Companies Act demands more advanced and complex accounting from a company than is the case for a sole trader, and the company's accounts must be audited. So, professional help will certainly be needed.

capital allowances and losses: limited company
These are the same for companies as for sole traders and partnerships, but cannot be set off against the directors' or shareholders' income from other sources: they apply only to the company's income.

A trading loss in any one period may be set off retrospectively, against the previous year's profit only; claims must be made within 2 years. Or else the loss may be carried forward to offset the profits of subsequent years; the period in which losses may be carried forward is indefinite, but the claims must be made within 6 years.

accounting period: limited company

A company may choose any date it likes for its accounting period. Corporation tax is, however, charged by reference to the fiscal financial year which runs from 1st April to 31st March and if (as is often the case) the company's accounting period is different, then the trading profits of two periods will be apportioned on a time basis. For instance, if a company has chosen January to December as its accounting period, then the apportionment will take 9/12 of trading profits of one period and 3/12 of the following one. Other income and any capital gains are not apportioned; their actual date decides which fiscal financial year they come into.

Tax is due 9 months from the end of the accounting period (that is, September in the case of a January to December accounting period) or 30 days after the Inland Revenue have issued an assessment, whichever is the later.

VAT CHANGES IN 1987–88

Cash accounting scheme: a new option available from 1 October 1987 to all firms whose taxable turnover (including VAT) does not exceed 250,000. Under this scheme, VAT accounts are rendered, not on the basis of the tax invoices, but on the basis of money actually paid and received. This offers special advantages to businesses giving extended credit to customers – they need not account for VAT on credit transactions until they have received payment, and they enjoy automatic bad debt relief.

Once-a-year VAT returns: another option which is due to operate from summer 1988.

For details of these schemes, contact your local VAT office.

---

value added tax (VAT)

This is a tax payable quarterly, not to the Inland Revenue but to HM Customs and Excise, on the supply of most goods and services in Great Britain. It consists of input and output tax. There are two kinds of registration: compulsory and voluntary.

The tax you pay on goods and services that you buy for your business is called *input tax*: the tax you charge your customers is called *output tax*. At present, both are 15 per cent.

This is how it works: Bill buys raw materials for £230, inclusive of 15 per cent VAT; £30 is his input tax. He uses the materials to manufacture products selling for £450, exclusive of 15 per cent VAT. So the selling price would amount to £517.50 of which £67.50 is his output tax. He deducts the input tax from it, and remits the balance (£37.50) to Customs and Excise. If his input tax had been greater than his output tax, he would have been refunded the difference.

At present there are 3 categories of goods and services:

(1) *exempt:* on which no VAT is payable under any circumstances (for example, insurance, doctors' services)
(2) *zero-rated:* on which, in theory, tax is payable but, in practice, none is paid, because the tax rate is zero per cent (for example, exported goods, food in shops, books)
(3) *standard-rated:* on which VAT at 15 per cent is charged. The figure is liable to change at the government's decision.

The difference between (1) and (2) may seem trivial, but is actually important. You cannot claim refunds of input tax unless you are collecting output tax, if only notionally. If you dealt only in exempt supplies, you would not be a 'taxable person', and could not be registered for VAT. You could then not recover any of the input tax you paid on your supplies, such as telephone charges and stationery, any more than a private person can.

However, this is not the case if you deal only in zero-rated supplies (for example, if you are an exporter). You can claim refunds of your input tax – unless you exercise a zero-rated option of trader's exemption from VAT, in which case you lose these refunds.

compulsory registration

You must register for VAT if your taxable turnover is likely to exceed £21,300 in the year in which you start trading or, if you have already started trading and at the end of the first quarter your taxable turnover is more than £7,250. Even if you go over the limit for the first quarter, you will not have to register if you can convince Customs and Excise that your trade is seasonal, and that you will therefore not exceed the £21,300 limit for the four quarters together. (But if you were to be wrong about this yourself, it could be an expensive mistake for you.)

Trade in zero-rated supplies counts towards your turnover, but not trade in exempt supplies.

If you buy a going concern from a VAT-registered trader, you must be registered too – and may be allowed to go on using the same VAT registration number. (If you decide VAT registration is not to your advantage, perhaps if you intend to run the business on a smaller scale, you can apply for deregistration.) You should get your registration in order before you sign the contract to buy the business. There is a leaflet (700/9/85) available from your VAT office, about buying a going concern.

To register, contact your local VAT office, at Customs and Excise, who will send you forms to fill up. Once you have done this, you must immediately start charging your customers VAT and keeping records, without waiting to be alloted a registration number) because you yourself will be charged VAT from the moment you become liable for registration. So it is best not to get into arrears, which you may find it difficult to recover from your customers in retrospect. And it is worth setting up a system from the very beginning because it is hard to do 12 months' books in arrears.

You must keep records of all transactions: do not make guesses. Keep for inspection all invoices you receive which show payment of VAT. You have to make quarterly returns showing your input and output tax, and to submit to having your VAT records inspected at intervals. There are civil penalties for defaulting on payments.

voluntary registration

With a turnover under £21,300 a year, you may still apply for registration if you are able to convince Customs and Excise that this is necessary for the health of your business.

Some of the advantages of registration are:

○ You can claim back all your input tax (for instance, on equipment you have to buy when setting up). This is especially advantageous if your goods or services are zero-rated.

○ If you start trading unregistered and your turnover grows to the point where you have to register, the addition of VAT will increase all your prices: this will dismay your customers, if they are consumers and not registered traders, and so cannot claim back the increase.

○ VAT can ease your cash flow difficulties. If you arrange to make major purchases just before you are due to make out a return, your input VAT will be refunded shortly after you get the invoice, even though you may be receiving 3 months' credit from your suppliers. (But this scheme will work against you if you yourself give credit to customers: you will have to pay your output VAT months before you yourself get paid.)

Some of the disadvantages of registration are:

○ The record-keeping and accounting demanded by VAT are an addition to your labours which you may not welcome if you employ a small office staff, or none. Matters become still more complicated if you deal in a variety of goods, some standard-rated and others zero-rated, for example, stationery and books.

○ If you are an exporter, you must be able to prove (by means of the relevant shipping documents) that your goods were, in fact, sold abroad. If some of your trade is in export and some is home trade, you will have the complication of selling goods differently rated.

HOW TO BE AN EMPLOYER

Yes, there is such a thing as a one-man business, particularly if what is being offered is a service or a consultancy. A plumber or electrician, for instance, needs only a telephone-answering machine to record customers' calls: he calls them back in the evenings, and does his book-keeping on sundays.

Many small firms start up with no other staff than the entrepreneur himself and his family, or a partner. But unless the family is large and willing, the firm will soon be needing some other employees, if it is to achieve progress.

In fact, a manufacturing business is likely to need employees from the start. It may only be a case of a couple of part-timers, or outworkers, or one trained secretary; even so, the businessman immediately becomes an employer, and should find out how to go about it.

finding and recruiting staff
When you have decided to take on employees, start by defining exactly what their duties are to be and what experience, skills and qualities are required to do the job. Avoid the temptation to ask for experience and qualifications greater than are necessary. This will make it easier for you to find the right person and easier, also, for any applicant to decide whether the job is the right one for him or her. A good working relationship is much more likely to develop if both you and your workers are well suited to each other.

Ways of finding suitable employees include the public employment service (jobcentre or careers office, both listed in the telephone directory), employment agencies (which charge the employer a fee), personal recommendation or advertisements in your local or national or trade press or local radio stations.

If you have a shop or factory with an entrance on the main road, place an advertisement where it can be seen by passers-by. Or advertise for new workers by placing cards in local shops. This is cheap and generally produces a good response. Specify exactly what is wanted – and if you are willing to train new staff, make this clear.

It is sometimes easier and more economical to employ more casual, part-time or freelance workers than full-time permanent staff, particularly when employing young mothers who are keen to get jobs which can be done partly at home, or with flexible hours, perhaps not coming into work during school holidays.

It can be a bad mistake to employ acquaintances; this can prove embarrassing if they turn out to be no good. Also, do not try to recruit staff when you already have large orders and are very busy. This would be inefficient because it does not allow time for training.

Remember that any advertisement, wherever it is placed, must not exclude anyone on grounds of race or sex, except in a very few closely defined cases.

Local jobcentres provide a fast, free recruitment service for all types of jobs, and jobcentre staff can advise on selection and can provide general information on employment legislation.

You may decide to employ young people and train them yourself: the government offers some financial incentives to firms willing to help reduce unemployment among school leavers. Consult your local careers service office or jobcentre about this and for advice on training.

If you are looking for a worker with a particular skill which is in short supply locally, your local jobcentre can give a wide circulation to the vacancy, to attract workers from other areas.

A worker with a particular skill may be already employed elsewhere and you may need to offer him terms that are in some way an improvement on what he is getting or can get in his present job, in order to attract him away. If he is at present employed locally, make sure his contract of employment does not prohibit him from leaving to take up a similar job within, say, five miles of his existing place of employment, otherwise he and you could end up with a costly court case.

If you ask for references, be sure to take them up, preferably by telephone. The previous employer will probably prove more frank in speaking to you in confidence, than in writing. A particularly glowing reference always provokes the suspicion that the previous employers are anxious to part with its subject.

paying wages and salaries

Most new businesses set their own rates of pay, depending on how much they expect to be able to afford. However, in some trades and industries, such as certain sectors of retailing, catering, hairdressing and clothing manufacture, wages councils are empowered to fix legally enforceable minimum rates of pay (a basic rate and an overtime rate) for employees aged 21 and over.

It is a criminal offence for employers in these trades and industries to pay their workers less than the minimum. It is the job of the Wages Inspectorate's inspectors to enforce these minimum rates. The Wages Act 1986 also requires employers to display notices of wages orders where the workers can see them, and to keep wage and time records, to show that they are complying with the law. For more information, contact your local office of the Wages Inspectorate: if you do not know where this is, ▲ get in touch with the Head Office at Gatliffe House, 93 Ebury Bridge Road, London SW1W 8RE (telephone: 01-730 6105/9 and 9161/7).

Another factor affecting wage levels may be an agreement between the employers' federation of your trade and the appropriate trade unions, which may be binding on you. If there are similar businesses in the area, it is wise to find out what they are paying, and if it is related to a union rate. Men and women doing the same or broadly similar work are, of course, entitled to the same rates of pay.

Your accountant will tell you how to set up a wages book, and may even agree, for a fee, to look after your payroll until you are sufficiently organised to take care of it yourself.

avoiding employment disputes

The independent Advisory, Conciliation and Arbitration Service (ACAS) can be consulted on matters relating to employment and industrial relations. Though this organisation is mostly known to the public as conciliators in industrial disputes or disputes between individuals and their employers, a considerable part of its work is preventive and consists of advising both sides of industry on industrial relations matters, including finding their way through the complications of employment legislation. All ACAS services are free.

▲ The ACAS head office is at 11 St. James's Square, London SW1Y 4LA: offices in Scotland, Wales and seven English regions deal with written and telephone enquiries. Visits to employers' premises by ACAS advisers can be arranged, and free booklets are available about recruitment and selection, workplace communications, job evaluation, and other aspects of employment.

Some small businessmen are unreasonably frightened of employing anyone – so much so, that they stunt their firm's growth by not taking on the necessary staff. But the acrimonious industrial disputes featured in the newspapers and on TV seldom affect the small businesses, which have, as a rule, good industrial relations. This may be because workers and 'boss' work in close contact with each other and have a common interest in making the firm do well.

This does not mean, of course, that as a small employer you are exempt from the laws enacted to protect the employee. On the contrary, if you want to promote harmony, you will attend to them scrupulously: the most important ones are those concerned with hiring, firing and working conditions.

rights of employees
It is important for new entrepreneurs not to be unsure about the rights of employees, under current legislation. ACAS has produced three codes of practice (obtainable from HMSO): *Disciplinary practice and procedures in employment; Disclosure of information to trade unions for collective bargaining purposes;* and *Time off for trade union duties and activities*. It has also produced a guide to employment particularly intended for the small business called *Employing people* (free from ACAS offices). In addition, ask at any jobcentre or unemployment benefit office for a series (1–16) of Department of Employment booklets on employment legislation, which cover between them every topic that you should be informed about. Only a brief outline can be given here.

written details of employment terms *(booklet 1)*

Every employee who works for you full-time (or part-time for more than 16 hours a week), must by law be provided, within 13 weeks of starting work, with a written statement setting out the conditions and terms on which he is employed. (This is sometimes called a 'contract of employment' though that is not strictly correct: the contract was formed earlier, when you made someone a firm offer of a job and it was firmly accepted. This is legally enforceable as soon as an employee starts work.)

The written statement must contain information on at least these points:

○ name of the employer and employee
○ whether employment with a previous employer counts as part of continuous period of employment
○ date of starting employment
○ title or description of employee's job
○ rates of pay (including overtime, if any) and how they are calculated
○ whether payment is to be by cheque, cash or bank transfer
○ times when payment is made (weekly or monthly)
○ hours of work (regular and overtime, if applicable)
○ holidays and holiday pay
○ sick pay arrangements
○ pension scheme arrangements and whether a contracting-out certificate under the Social Security Pensions Act 1975 is in force
○ length of notice required from employer and from employee
○ rules relating to disciplinary procedures, such as warnings and dismissal, and procedure for taking up grievances.

If any of these points do not apply, for instance if there are no pension arrangements, the document must say so explicitly.

It is the practice of many employers to confirm an oral offer of job by a letter, setting out the conditions and terms. If all these above points are covered, such a letter will do in place of a written statement; if they are not, a written statement will still be necessary.

Part-time workers employed for less than 16 hours and more than 8 hours a week are also entitled to a written statement of employment, but only after they have worked for you for 5 years – but, of course, you do not have to wait till then.

The terms set out in the statement cannot be altered without the consent of both parties. If you transfer the employee to another kind of work or promote him, he no longer has the same job and may need a new written statement.

itemised pay statements *(booklet 8)*
With each wage payment, you must give each employee a wage slip showing his gross pay, deductions (with the reason given for each, such as income tax, National Insurance contributions, union dues), and the net pay.

You will, of course, keep a copy of this for your own records. If you pay wages in cash, get your copy signed by the employee, as a receipt.

guarantee payments *(booklet 9)*
If business is bad, you may want to put some employees on short time, or even lay them off, without pay, or with pay at a lower rate. Your right to do so should be specified at the time of engaging an employee. You should also be aware that most employees are entitled to a guarantee payment for up to five working days in any three months in which you have no work for them to do.

Consult also *booklet 11: Rules governing continuous employment*. It is particularly important, because it explains what 'continuous employment' means in law: many employees' rights depend on their being continuously employed.

time off work for public duties *(booklet 12)*
You should allow time off (sometimes with pay) to employees engaged on public duties: for example, justices of the peace, local councillors, school managers or governors.

maternity entitlements (booklet 4)

A pregnant employee has the right to time off without loss of pay for visits to antenatal clinics. Where an employee is leaving work to have a baby and has worked for you for at least 2 years (or five years if she works between 8 and 16 hours a week) up to the eleventh week before her confinement (and fulfils certain other qualifying conditions), you must give her at least 90 per cent of her normal pay, less the standard rate of maternity allowance, whether or not she receives this, for the first 6 weeks of her absence – whether or not she is coming back to work for you. You can claim a full rebate for this from the Maternity Pay Fund (administered by the Department of Employment's redundancy payments offices) provided you were actually liable to pay maternity pay to the employee.

If your employee fulfils the qualifying conditions, she is entitled to come back to work for you in her former job (or a suitable alternative where it is not reasonably practical for you to offer her the former job) at any time up to the end of the 29th week after the birth of the child. But she must tell you this (in writing, at least 21 days before her absence begins) and must produce a certificate of expected confinement, if you want to see it. Not earlier than 49 days after the expected confinement, you may write to ask her if she still intends to return and she must reply within 14 days and must let you know the date on which she wants to return at least 21 days in advance.

when employees fall ill

Under the statutory sick pay scheme, which has replaced the old sickness benefit, an employer must pay his employees statutory sick pay (SSP) for up to 28 weeks' illness. Spells of illness shorter than 4 days (including sundays and holidays) do not qualify for sick pay. The 28-week maximum 'period of incapacity for work' is not limited to one tax year: it may be made up of intermittent periods of illness, provided that the gap between any of these is not more than eight weeks. When an employee's illness, whether 'linked' or continuous, lasts longer than 28 weeks, your obligation ceases and state benefit takes over; but your obligation starts again if, having recovered, she should fall ill again more than eight weeks after the end of a maximum period.

You do not stand to lose by paying SSP: each month you can recover what you have paid out by deducting it from that month's total of National Insurance contributions, before forwarding the balance to the Inland Revenue.

For a detailed explanation of the rules, consult the DHSS booklet NI 227, *Employer's guide to statutory sick pay*, available from your DHSS office.

dismissing an employee

It is essential for every employer to know exactly when and in what circumstances he may dismiss an employee.

Going about it the wrong way can lead to a complaint of unfair dismissal to an industrial tribunal, and if this body finds against you, it has the power to order re-employment of, or an award of compensation to, the employee. Such an award can be crippling to a small business; what is more, you will in most cases have to pay the costs of defending yourself, win or lose.

You cannot just sack an employee on the spot, however provoked you may be. An employee who has worked for you for four weeks or more is entitled to a week's notice or a week's salary in lieu of notice unless his contract of employment specified a longer period of notice. After two years, he must have one week's notice for each year of working for you, up to a maximum of 12 weeks. Every employee working 16 hours or more a week, who has been employed for six months or more, is entitled to a written statement of the reason why he is being dismissed, if he asks for one. In a firm employing fewer than 20 people, a statement of reason for dismissal need only be given to someone who has been employed there for two years or more.

Except in the case of wholly intolerable misconduct, it is unwise to dismiss anyone for a first offence. Put yourself in the right by discussing the matter with the employee and listening to what he has to say. An employer must make proper investigations into any suspicion of misconduct and allow his employee to state his side of the case and to bring along someone to represent him.

It is important to send him a written warning, explaining exactly what fault you find with his work and/or conduct, and demanding that he mend his ways – or risk dismissal.

If there is no improvement, send a second warning, and, if necessary, a third, keeping copies of all of them; after this you are fairly safe in giving notice without the risk of a complaint of unfair dismissal succeeding against you provided that you can prove the facts leading to the dismissal.

industrial tribunal

A dismissed employee who started work on or after 1st June 1985 may bring a complaint of unfair dismissal to an industrial tribunal only after a minimum of two years' continuous employment. (Those who started work before that date have been able to bring a complaint after only one year, except in the case of small firms, employing 20 or fewer people, where the two year rule still applies.) However, there is no qualifying period for employees who allege that they were dismissed because of trade union activity.

The industrial tribunal will take account of the firm's size and resources when deciding whether a dismissal was fair or not, and whether to direct re-employment. For instance, if a worker has proved not up to the physical demands of the job, a small firm may not have another job to offer him, and may therefore dismiss him.

Consult *booklet 13, Unfairly dismissed?* and *booklet 14, Rights to notice and reasons for dismissal.* Other useful publications of the Department of Employment are: *Fair and unfair dismissal: a guide for employers*, and *The law on unfair dismissal: guidance for small firms*.

making employees redundant

Employees may have to be made redundant when a firm is not doing enough business to justify their employment. A redundancy dismissal can be unfair on the basis of improper selection, lack of consultation and lack of notice. It should certainly not be motivated by personal reasons. A worker who thinks you are making him redundant just to get rid of him can challenge your decision before an industrial tribunal.

Anyone whom you have employed continuously for two years is entitled to redundancy pay, the amount of which will depend on the person's rate of pay and length of employment. Some of this money (at present 35 per cent) will be refunded by the Department of Employment, whose advice you should seek if you have to cope with redundancies. (See *booklet 16: Redundancy payments.*)

There is an obligation on the employer to inform his local Department of Employment if he is going to make ten or more people redundant, otherwise he will lose his rebate. You will find the address of your local office in the telephone directory.

An employee with two years' continuous employment (or five years' part-time employment) who is being made redundant, is entitled to time off with pay to look for or to train for other work. Consult *booklet 2: Procedure for handling redundancies,* and *booklet 6: Facing redundancy? Time off for job hunting.*

One important point to be aware of if you take over a going concern, is that workers' employment is deemed in law to be continuing. So if you decide to replace some of them, you may find yourself with a good deal of compensation to pay, even though you did not hire these people, and they have not worked for you very long. This is one of the dangers of taking over a going concern, so before you do so, ask for a roll of employees, showing their length of continuous employment there, so that you can assess the amount of possible redundancy pay.

Look also at *booklet 10: Employment rights on transferring an undertaking.* If you know in advance that you will want to make employees redundant, negotiate with the seller of the business about which of you is to pay.

other points to bear in mind
If any of your employees are members of a trade union, you will do well to read *booklet 7: Union membership rights and the closed shop.* Note also that a trade union official may legitimately ask for time off for his duties: this is covered by an ACAS code of practice.

The question of sex discrimination in employment can be studied in the Home Office publication *Sex discrimination: a guide to the Sex Discrimination Act 1975,* obtainable from jobcentres.

The Consumer Publication *Taking your own case to court or tribunal* deals, amongst other things, with taking a claim of unfair dismissal or redundancy to an industrial tribunal.

A two-day course on employment law is amongst the courses organised by The Industrial Society, Peter Runge House, 3 ▲ Carlton House Terrace, London SW1Y 5DG (telephone: 01-839 4300). Some of their other courses range from 'Achieving people's commitment at work' to 'Understanding financial information'.

health and safety of employees

The responsibilities concerning the health, safety and welfare of people at work are defined in broad terms by the Health and Safety at Work etc Act 1974. It places important general duties on all people at work – employers, employees and the self-employed, manufacturers, suppliers, designers and importers of materials used at work, and people in control of premises. More detailed and specific requirements for particular kinds of work are laid down by other legislation, such as the Offices Shops and Railways Premises Act 1963 which specifies what must be provided in the way of washrooms, lavatories, heat, ventilation and light, somewhere to sit, and so on. The Factories Act 1961 and other statutes and regulations apply to many different work activities.

The requirements to protect health and safety and provide welfare vary considerably depending on the type of work being carried on. You will need to find out how your business will be affected and what facilities and safeguards you must provide in matters such as machinery guards, protective clothing, storage and handling of dangerous substances.

If in doubt, consult the appropriate enforcing authority – who may come to inspect your premises. Generally, the enforcing authority is the local authority for most shops, offices, hotel and catering activities. For other businesses, it is the Health and Safety Executive, whose factory inspectorate must be notified of any premises to be used as a factory, at least 28 days beforehand.

Addresses of local authority enforcement offices can be obtained from district council offices or, in case of difficulty, from the local authority liaison officer in the nearest HSE area office. There are some 20 such offices, and three regional enquiry points:

▲ Baynards House, 1 Chepstow Place, London W2 4TF (telephone: 01-221 0870); Broad Lane, Sheffield S3 7HQ (telephone: 0742-752539) and St. Hugh's House, Stanley Precinct, Trinity Road, Bootle L20 3QY (telephone: 051-951 4381).

The HSE publishes a range of explanatory and guidance material; some publications are available free of charge from HSE offices. The booklet *A guide to the HSW Act* (HS)(R)(6) is obtainable from HMSO or bookshops, at £2.75. Twice a year the HSE publishes a list of all its publications, and this is available free of charge from any of the three enquiry points.

With some computers, you may be able to get information about health and safety direct from HSELINE, the HSE database. There is also an 'electronic noticeboard', which gives the most up-to-date details of new publications and legislation. For further information, fees, etc., contact HSE at the Sheffield address. HSELINE is available on a number of host computers, and also compact disc read only memories (CDROM).

All accidents at work must be recorded and all serious ones, which lead to having 3 or more days off or at least one day in hospital, must be reported on a special form to the local Health and Safety Executive. Near-miss accidents must also be reported. Every place of work should have a well-equipped first aid box, the contents of which are specified, and the employees should know where it is kept and there should be someone trained to use it.

agent for the government

You are the channel by which your employees' PAYE income tax is transmitted to the Board of Inland Revenue, as well as their National Insurance contributions (and yours, too).

Leaflet IR 53, *Thinking of taking someone on?*, obtainable from the Inspector of Taxes and from PAYE enquiry offices, explains and clearly illustrates the procedure.

coping with PAYE

If you employ anyone in your business in return for wages, even members of your own family, you are responsible for deducting their income tax at source and sending it to the Inland Revenue every month (even if you pay wages weekly). As soon as you hire someone, let your tax office know: you will be told which is to be your PAYE office.

An employee who has previously been employed and paid tax should bring you his form P45 which has on it his code number and total pay and total tax to date in the financial year. A new employee who has not paid PAYE tax before, must be given form P46 which you can get from the Inland Revenue office, and an emergency code number.

The tax inspector will send you two sets of printed tables, *Free pay table A*, and PAYE *taxable pay tables B–D*. By looking up each code number in the tables, you will know how much tax to deduct each week or month. You enter the amount, the gross salary and other details on each employee's deductions working sheet, which has a space for each week of the tax year.

At the end of the tax year, all the information concerning each employee's wages, income tax and National Insurance contributions must be entered on a triplicate form (P14), two copies of which are sent to the collector of taxes who passes one of them on to the DHSS; the third (certificate P60) goes to the employee.

National Insurance

As an employer, you are also responsible for collecting all your employees' National Insurance contributions every week or month, together with their income tax, and sending them on to Inland Revenue (not the DHSS) together with yours, the employer's contributions. You work out the contributions from tables supplied by Inland Revenue.

Arrangements exist for employees to contract out of part of their contributions where a firm has an occupational pension scheme, but this is unlikely to concern you at this stage.

You will be concerned with 3 kinds of contributions, as listed:

National Insurance contributions (as from April 1987)

Type of contri- bution	Category of insured person	Basis of contri- bution	Earnings limits lower	upper	Amount paid
Class 1	employed earners	earnings- related	£39.00 a week	£295 a week (employees only)	variable, up to 9% employee 10.45% employer
Class 2	self- employed	flat rate	—	—	£3.85 a week
Class 4	self- employed	earnings- related	£4,590 annual profits	£15,340	6.3% of amount by which profits exceed lower imit, up to £677.25 p.a.

class 1 contributions

These are due from each of your employees who is over sixteen and below the minimum pension age (65 for a man, 60 for a woman) whose earnings reach the lower earnings limit. For each of them, you must pay the employer's share. (Contributions are not due from employees over pension age, but you must continue to pay the employer's share.) Obviously the lower earnings limit figure is one to bear in mind when employing part-time staff. If you go over this limit, both the employee and you have to pay National Insurance contributions, and an apparently generous pay increase may prove a lot less lavish after extra deductions for National Insurance and tax.

If yours is a limited company, you as an individual pay an employee's share, and the company pays the employer's contribution – although in effect, in a small company you would be paying both the sums.

class 2 contributions

You pay these if you are a sole trader or a partner, and there are some benefits from which you are excluded, notably unemployment benefit. You can claim exemption from class 2 payments if you are able to show that your net earnings from self-employment in a tax year are expected to be below a certain sum (£2,225 in 1987/8). You must apply to the DHSS for a certificate of exemption in advance. The certificate cannot normally be back-calculated, and any contributions already paid cannot be refunded.

If you start your business in your spare time while continuing to work for an employer, you must pay both class 1 and class 2 contributions. There is, however, an upper limit, and anything you pay over this amount in a tax year will be refunded to you.

There are several ways of paying. You can buy a stamp every week at a post office, and stick it on a contribution card which your local DHSS office will send you; or you can arrange to pay by direct debit, through your bank or National Girobank.

class 4 contributions

These are payable by class 2 payers whose taxable profits exceed a certain sum; there is an upper limit on the amount payable.

Class 4 contributions are assessed together with income tax by the Inland Revenue. If you expect your contributions to go over the set limits in any year, you can apply to defer the payment till your earnings have been assessed for tax. 50 per cent of your class 4 contributions may now be offset against your gross earnings for tax relief.

For fuller information about National Insurance, go directly to the source, the DHSS. Leaflets, updated every year, to be consulted include the following:

NI40   *National Insurance Guide for Employees*
NP15   *Employer's Guide to National Insurance Contributions*
NI208 *National Insurance Contribution Rates*
NI41   *National Insurance Guide for the Self-employed*
NP28   *More Than One Job? (Class 1 Contributions)*
NP18   *Class 4 NI Contributions*
NI27A *People with small earnings from self-employment*
NI35   *National Insurance for Company Directors*

INSURANCE FOR THE SMALL BUSINESS

When you are just starting up in business and every penny counts, having to pay insurance premiums can seem to be an uncalled-for imposition. But you would see this in a different light if the occasion arose to put in a claim. Then you might start to worry whether you had taken enough insurance to cover all the losses you had suffered.

Insurance is best thought of as the price of peace of mind. Calamities will happen, as everyone knows. Make sure, if you take out insurance, that the cover is adequate – otherwise, you might as well not bother.

Almost every aspect of trading can create a need for some kind of insurance. For most kinds you can find cover, but sometimes the premium may be high.

The premiums paid for any business insurance are deductible expenses which can be set off against tax.

employer's liability insurance

The law requires that everyone on your payroll (except for members of your family and domestic servants) must be covered by this insurance, and that a current certificate of insurance be displayed at the place of work.

The employer's liability insurance covers you for claims that might arise because an employee suffered physical injury or illness in the course of, or resulting from, his employment. This could be anything from a twisted ankle after falling down stairs to losing a limb. It would be necessary for the employee suing you for damages to show that the injury or illness arose not from his own inadvertence, but out of your negligence or that of another employee.

You would be wise to include employed members of the family in the insurance cover, even though you do not need to. Close relationship does not preclude a claim for damages, and if one of your nearest and dearest were to suffer, you would be glad to have them compensated by the insurance company.

Most insurance companies will quote you rates for this type of insurance. The premiums are related to the size of your payroll and will also depend on the risks attached to the jobs. If your employees do office work only, it is likely to cost less than if they work with machinery or shift heavy loads.

▲ The Health & Safety Executive, 1 Chepstow Place, London W2 4TF (telephone: 01-221 0870/0416) has published a small brochure *Short Guide to the Employer's Liability (Compulsory Insurance) Act 1969* (HSE 4), which is available free on request. Their publications are also available from the following enquiry points: HSE, St.
▲ Hugh's House, Stanley Precinct, Trinity Road, Bootle, Merseyside L20 3QY (telephone: 051-951 4381) and HSE Library and Information Service, Broad Lane, Sheffield S3 7HQ (telephone: 0742-768141/752539).

material damage insurance
You would be foolhardy not to insure for the various disasters that could mean the rapid end of your business, such as burglary, fire, flood, subsidence, malicious damage, explosion, to name but a few. Some of the features of a business that should be covered are

- the business premises (including site clearance and rebuilding costs)
- their contents (including fixtures and fittings, industrial plant, tools and other equipment)
- the stock (including supplies not yet used and goods that have been allocated to customers, even if the customer has not yet paid for them)
- goods in transit (on the way to the customer, or to a sub-contractor, or to the docks for shipment; in your own or someone else's vehicles; sent by post)
- goods on a sub-contractor's premises.

You could take out a separate policy for each kind of risk, but it would be more efficient to have a single material damage insurance policy covering them all.

Many trade associations arrange (or act as agents for) special insurance policies tailored for the needs of the particular trade.

The insurance should be revised and updated at regular intervals, otherwise you might find a huge discrepancy between the amount you are covered for and what your loss actually amounts to if you need to make a claim.

consequential loss insurance

This is a corollary to material damage insurance: it covers further losses which would arise if your business were to come to a standstill following a disaster that is covered by the insurance. Should your premises burn down, for instance, you would not only need to rebuild and re-equip but would also have to pay your wage bill and some overhead costs while no money is coming in. You may have lost all your stock and your office records and files, and by the time you are back in business, your customers may have gone elsewhere.

Consequential loss insurance should cover all these situations, loss of profit, and your overhead costs for a limited period (known as the indemnity period). Usually this is not less than 12 months; you may be able to negotiate a longer period, and the particular features of your business may need other special terms.

public liability insurance

Apart from the statutory insurance for liability to employees, there is insurance to cover you for claims by members of the public who have been injured as a result of your (or one of your employees') activities at work: for example, a brick dropped from a scaffolding on a passer's-by head.

product liability insurance

This covers you for claims arising out of faults in something you or your employees have manufactured or serviced – if your folding chair collapses under a purchaser, say, or the washing machine you have repaired gives a severe electrical shock.

insurance for car and driver
Third-party insurance is, of course compulsory on all the firm's vehicles; and you should insure at the same time for theft and accidents, etc. If your vehicles are going to be driven by various persons, make sure yours is an all-drivers policy.

If your work involves a great deal of driving, you would be wise to insure for loss of your driving licence, which could otherwise mean the loss of your livelihood. The insurance cannot restore your licence, but it can supply the means to hire a chauffeur.

insurance if money is lost
A policy of this sort will cover you for loss of money (including cheques and postal orders) from your office, your till, from your house, or in transit – for instance, you could be robbed while taking it to the bank. Insurance can also be taken out to compensate an employee who is injured while being robbed of money.

Firms who hold clients' money, such as travel agents or insurance agents, need an insurance bond to protect them against loss if the business fails. Bonding is compulsory for some types of agency.

personal insurance
You might consider private health insurance. One reason would be that if you were confined to bed in hospital, you would have a room to yourself, and a telephone, and could keep in touch with your business to an extent impossible in a public ward. You could have some control over the timing of a non-urgent operation, so that it coincided with a slack business period, for example.

If you start a business alone, without a partner, an illness or accident which takes you out of circulation for any length of time could be damaging – or fatal – to your prospects. You can take out a policy to cover these contingencies.

There is also a 'key person' insurance under which a limited company, a partnership or sole proprietor can obtain cover for loss of profit suffered as the consequence of the death of the proprietor, managing director, partner or senior employee. Any claim would be met either by a single lump sum or a number of annual instalments for some years following the death of the key person.

It is possible to get insurance to cover the cost of replacement personnel if a key person is called for jury service.

In a partnership, it is possible to get insurance for the eventuality of having to buy the partner's share in the business from his inheritors, in the event of the partner's death.

other insurance

There is hardly a calamity for which you cannot insure your business or yourself. For instance, if you have a shop, you might enquire about a plate glass insurance policy, which would provide such facilities as having your broken window and/or door boarded up, speedy replacement of the glass, compensation for damage or injury by shattered glass, consequential loss of profits.

You can insure to cover you being robbed or defrauded by your employees; you can even insure in case you are made to pay compensation by an industrial tribunal.

▲ By becoming a member of the National Federation of Self-Employed and Small Businesses Limited, 140 Lower Marsh, London SE1 7AE (telephone: 01-928 9272), you are automatically entitled to insurance cover of up to £25,000 in these specific areas: expenses of VAT tribunal cases; awards made by industrial tribunals; Inland Revenue in-depth investigations and appeals against decisions under the 1985 Finance Act in respect of VAT. Further legal expenses insurance includes assistance with HSE cases, and motoring prosecutions, and a further benefit is a 24-hour telephone legal advice service.

The Federation has over 50,000 members nationally, and is serviced by eight professionally staffed offices across the country. Membership is open to individuals who are self-employed, partners in a firm, or owners or directors of a small business.

brokers

You can never insure against anything, only for the cash compensation for any loss that you may suffer as a result of a happening. Insurance is a major industry, complex and rather specialised, so there may be a case for getting the advice of an insurance broker specialising in commercial insurance, particularly if you need some unusual type of insurance or if you are faced with what seem excessively high premium demands.

▲ To find a good insurance broker, personal recommendation is likely to be best; or you might get in touch with BIBA, the British Insurance Brokers' Association, BIBA House, 14 Bevis Marks, London EC3A 7NT (telephone: 01-623 9043) and ask for the names of some brokers willing to serve a small business, and make your choice from these. BIBA also offers a free leaflet, *We've got a small firms' policy just for you*, which gives a brief checklist of the types of insurance that a small business may need.

TIME TO GET A COMPUTER?

The justification for getting a computer is to increase the efficiency of your business at least enough to offset the cost of installing and running the computer.

To assess your needs, start by making a list of all the areas in which a computer could be used in your business – for example, routine letters and circulars, costings, estimates and quotations, book-keeping and accounts, invoices and statements, financial planning (including cash flow and profit and loss forecasting), stock control, payrolls (including PAYE and National Insurance).

If your list shows that there would be plenty of work to do on the computer, it is worth going to the next stage: searching out the right system and costing it. If the list is only short or the benefit not clear, put off any decision, but keep the list going and plan to look at it in six months' or a year's time.

finding out about computers

Ideally, you should call in a consultant (not a salesman for a firm who may know only about his own type which, of course, he is intent on selling you). Tell him how your business works: "This is my business, these are the things I do, in which aspects could a computer help me, which computer and what should I buy – do I need a computer at all?" The cost of a consultant would be around £50–£75 an hour.

You could entrust the task of finding out about computers to a business partner, or someone else whom you trust and who knows your business; or, most probably, you will need to buff up on computers yourself. Even if you are letting someone else make recommendations, it is important that you yourself know something about computers, so that when it comes to making decisions, you will at least know what questions to ask and be able to follow the answers.

Sources of information on computers in business are:

o specialist shops (but bear in mind that they will want to push the machines and software that they stock). Chain stores selling computers are more home-computer oriented, and not the place from which to get information about a microcomputer for a business
o computer and business magazines and books; articles on computing in professional and trade magazines; exhibitions
o friends who work with computers
o small businesses who are already computerised
o courses in business computer appreciation or similar subjects, details of which you can obtain from the local technical colleges and advertisements in computer and business magazines. Some courses are quite short – one, two or three days (after all, you cannot afford to spend too much of your time away from your business, and the organisers of these courses realise this). There are also evening courses at colleges and universities
▲ o the government-sponsored National Computing Centre, details of which can be obtained from NCC, Oxford Road, Manchester M1 7ED (telephone: 061-228 6333)
▲ o the Federation of Microsystems Centres, an independent government-established body, with 20 centres located throughout the UK. Full details are obtainable from the Microsystems Administration Unit, Third Floor, Erick House, Princess Square, Newcastle-upon-Tyne NE1 8ER (telephone: 091-232 2353).

working out the cost
The cost of buying the computer itself, which can be anything from about £1,000 (at the moment – the costs change quite frequently), is just the start. You also have to allow for:

o software – which means the programs you want to use on the computer
o printer (choose one that can also be used as a typewriter, and if you are equipping your office from scratch, choose a typewriter that can become part of a computer system). If you do not mind

your clients knowing that your correspondence was produced by computer, a so-called dot-matrix printer is fast and versatile. For print that looks as though it was typed on an electric typewriter, you need a daisy-wheel printer: it gives better quality print, but is slower and less versatile and more expensive than a dot-matrix printer

○ stationery – floppy discs, computer paper, printer ribbon, etc

○ maintenance contract – one that guarantees you a replacement while your equipment is being repaired or serviced will cost between 10 and 50 per cent per year of the cost of buying the computer

○ training expenses for you (and partner/employees) learning to use the computer; possibly also temporary help in transferring all your information into the computer system when you first get it. Training courses are sometimes arranged as part of the software or hardware purchase deal.

Your starting figure, all in all, is unlikely to be less than £3,000, with average costs £6,500, but this depends on your individual requirements.

choosing the system
Begin with your software and then sort out an actual brand name of computer to run it on. If you want to get started with a couple of general purpose programs, and keep your options as wide as possible for adding specialised software later on, choose the software first, then the machine to run it. Get the hardware and software from the same place, which makes sense because you will then have the same outfit maintaining both.

Choose a computer that runs software on one of the popular operating systems. If there is no software specifically for your type of business, you should still be able to find software that meets most of your requirements.

You would almost certainly be able to make use of:

○ word processor: for producing, editing, storing and printing text. You can use it for letters and reports, mailing lists, printing standard forms (invoices, statements, orders etc), and so on

○ spreadsheet: takes the place of pencil, paper, rubber and calculator for producing, for example, cash flow forecasts, and trading and profit and loss accounts.

hardware

Hardware is the actual computer. There are scores of 'personal' computers to choose from, so narrow down your short list to half a dozen or so, and arrange for demonstrations. 'Personal' means a microcomputer for the use of one person (at a time), and implies something more than a 'home' computer which is not recommended for a business.

16 'bit' computers are now established as the norm for business use. You will need a computer with a double disc drive, and with one of the most common operating systems: MS DOS, CP/M86, Concurrent DOS, PC DOS, or UNIX for 16 bit computers.

data protection

The Data Protection Act was passed in 1984 following widespread concern about people's private affairs being recorded in computer databanks, with the attendant risks of inaccuracy and uncontrolled disclosure. Most of the provisions of the Act are now in force, and the rest will become so in November 1987.

It is a very wide-ranging piece of legislation, and yet its scope is in some ways restricted. It applies to all personal data about individuals (companies and organisations are excluded): not just sensitive information, but addresses and telephone numbers, even though these are to be found in directories. These data come under the Act if they are stored in some sort of mechanical device which can process them – for instance, a computer, word processor or punched card selection system. The address book and the ordinary card index are exempt.

If you have a computer, you may need to register under the Act. A number of uses are exempt, for example, the home computer used not for business but for family affairs, household accounts and so forth. In business, there are several exempt uses (calculating pay, keeping accounts or word processing) but the exemptions are hedged about with strict conditions. If any of these conditions are breached, the exemption is lost. It is often easier and safer to register than to rely on an exemption.

You must find out whether you will need to register. An explanatory booklet with application forms is available from post offices, or direct from the office of the Data Protection Registrar, ▲ Springfield House, Water Lane, Wilmslow, Cheshire SK9 5AX (telephone: 0625-525777).

You may need to register even if you do not have a computer of your own: your accountant, or a computer bureau may hold and process data for you, but you are their actual user. If you yourself have spare capacity on your computer which you make available to someone else, you will need to register as a computer bureau.

When registered, you must always operate within your registered particulars (such as purpose, type of data, source, to whom they are disclosed), and also in accordance with prescribed principles of good practice.

The register is open to public inspection. From 11 November 1987, any individual affected will be entitled to a copy of the information concerning him. Even now, anyone can claim compensation if his personal data are found to be inaccurate, lost, destroyed or improperly disclosed.

Many trade associations and chambers of commerce have been studying the requirements, and may be able to advise you; so, of course, can your professional advisers. Ask your accountant to add data protection to his checklist for your business, to make sure that you operate as registered, and/or to notify the Registrar of any changes.

The current fee for registration is £22. Registration lasts for 3 years, after which a renewal reminder will be sent automatically.

PROTECTING YOUR BUSINESS IDEA

If your business project is based on an original idea or invention of your own, you will naturally want to exploit it for your sole benefit for as long as possible.

There are various ways of protecting a business idea; which of them you choose depends on the nature of the idea and also on what you expect that your sole (monopoly) right to it will be worth. Protecting a business idea can be expensive, especially if the protection needs to be effective in several countries, so you must be sure that the resulting benefit will be worth the expense. There should be a sound commercial reason for seeking to establish a sole right.

Moreover, if this is infringed, your only redress lies in litigation, and that can be wasteful of time and money, whether you win or lose.

patents

A patent is the common way of establishing a legal claim to the ownership and sole exploitation of an invention. To be patent-able, an invention must be new, must constitute an inventive advance – that is, something more than just an obvious improve-ment on something already known or made – and must be capable of being used in industry or agriculture.

It is essential not to disclose its nature publicly to anyone, anywhere, before the patent application has been filed at the Patent Office. Once an idea has been made public, an application to patent it can be rejected on the grounds that it is no longer new; and even if the patent is granted, a business competitor may be able to get it revoked.

'patent applied for'

In the first stage of applying for a UK patent, you file an application
▲ (current fee £10) at the Patent Office (State House, 66–71 High
Holborn, London WC1R 4TP), together with a detailed description
and/or specification of your invention, and any necessary drawings. From the moment your application is received, you have
priority over anyone else's later application. You can then move
straight into the second stage, if you wish: this is often the
sensible thing to do. You have 12 months from the start of your
priority to decide whether to proceed, or to let your application
lapse. During that time the confidentiality of your application is
maintained.

If you decide to go ahead with stage 2, you must submit a claim
or set of claims, characterising the invention, and specifying the
scope of the protection to be granted. You must also submit an
abstract, that is, a shortened version, of your entire application,
and pay a fee (currently £85).

All the documentation is now passed to a technically qualified
examiner in the Patent Office, who makes a preliminary search in
the office records, and sends you a report listing any documents
or facts that might have a bearing on your application.

Stage 3 starts automatically about 18 months from the start of
the priority. The Patent Office notifies you that unless you choose
now to withdraw your application, the details of it will be
published and will no longer be confidential.

As soon as the invention is made public, any interested third
parties may write to the Patent Office, making objections to the
granting of a patent, on the grounds that it is not new or
inventive. They might, for instance, point out to the Patent Office
that you described your invention at a trade show months before
your application was filed.

You now have six months to decide whether to embark on
stage 4. If you do, you pay a fee (currently £100), and your
application is submitted to a yet more thorough scrutiny, to
ensure that it meets all the requirements for patentability.

The examiner will pursue any objections with you, until he is
satisfied. At any of the stages, you may be required (or you may

request) to make amendments; but you may not expand on what you originally claimed or on what was shown in your original drawings and descriptions. Thus all along you will have to make difficult decisions about coping with any improvements you may wish to make, or any amendments you may need to make. You may decide to withdraw altogether, or to introduce a fresh application and will have to consider all the commercial problems which may arise as a consequence.

When a UK patent is granted, it is published in its finally agreed form and runs for 20 years from the first date of application; however, it will lapse unless you pay renewal fees from the fifth year onwards. The current rates are between £78 and £320.

If you want to be also protected abroad, the time to apply is in the first twelve months. You can apply to patent your invention in several countries, and there are different ways of setting about it. You must always take care that you do not jeopardise an application by letting your application be published in one country during your confidential priority period in the others.

You can apply for a patent abroad in the country concerned; or, if the country is a member of the European Patent Convention or the more international Patent Co-operation Treaty, you can start your application at the Patent Office in London. European patents can be applied for at the European Patent Office in Munich.

how to go about it
You would be well advised to obtain the professional help of a patent agent, rather than to deal with a patent application yourself, unless you have considerable experience in that field. A confidential discussion with a patent agent should precede any disclosure of an idea to anyone at all. He will also be able to keep you informed about intended changes in the patent laws, and to help you decide what you must to do protect your position. Names, together with explanatory pamphlets, can be obtained from the Secretary, Chartered Institute of Patent Agents, Staple Inn Buildings, High Holborn, London WC1V 7PZ (telephone: 01-405 9450).

Patent Office pamphlets *Protecting innovation; Basic facts about patents for inventions in the UK; Introducing patents, a guide for inventors; Patents, a source of technical information; Counterfeiting;* a list of fees and the various forms required are available free from the Patent Office.

trade marks

The function of a trade mark is to identify the product as belonging to the owner of the mark (generally the manufacturer) and to distinguish his goods from those of others. A trade mark does not necessarily have to be registered, provided the owner can establish the use and reputation of the mark – which the owner of a new business is clearly unable to do. While registration of a trade mark is not mandatory in order to obtain protection for it at law, if the mark is currently registered under the Trade Mark Act 1938 it makes it much simpler for the owner to have recourse against any person infringing the mark or passing off his goods as those of the owner.

Trade marks may consist of a device (a picture or logo) and word or words, and signature, or some combination of these. A mark proposed for registration has to meet strict criteria in order to qualify. It must be distinctive, must not be deceptive, and must not be easily confused with other marks already registered in respect of similar kinds of goods; it must not describe or characterise the product, for example 'Tasty', and must not be a geographical name or a surname. So some trade marks proposed for registration are inherently unregistrable or have to be modified; others are unregistrable because a similar mark for similar sort of goods has already been registered.

applying for a trade mark
Application to register a trade mark (current fee £60) has to be made to the registrar of the Trade Marks Registry at the Patent Office who sees whether it complies with the provisions of the Trade Mark Act 1938. If it is considered acceptable, or will be acceptable after it has been modified, the mark is advertised in the

Trade Marks Journal. If no objections are raised by any third parties within a set period, it is entered in the register, upon payment of a further fee of £84, for an initial period of 7 years. After this, the mark may be renewed for periods of 14 years at a time (current fee £205), with no upper time limit to the registration.

Each trade mark application may refer to only one of the 34 classes of goods: if you want to use the same trade mark for several classes of goods, you must make a separate application for each class. A list of the classifications can be obtained from the registrar. A pamphlet entitled *Applying for a Trade Mark*, which lists fees, together with the necessary forms, is supplied without
▲ charge by the Trade Marks Registry at the Patent Office. The telephone number of the Patent Office is 01-831 2525.

service marks
From 1 October 1986 onwards, a service mark can be registered which identifies a service in the same way that a trade mark identifies a product. Some businesses may need to register both a trade mark and a service mark, representing different aspects of the business.

The same procedure should be followed as for trade mark applications. There are eight classes of services; the Trade Marks Registry will supply, on request, a pamphlet entitled *Applying for the registration of a service mark*, together with a list of fees and application forms.

protection abroad
To register a trade mark or service mark abroad, you must at present apply in each country in which you require protection. There are, however, proposals for the setting up of a central EEC trade and service marks registry.

You would be wise to apply for registration as early as possible, even before starting to trade abroad, because priority is allocated according to the date of filing the application. If someone beats you to it in filing a similar or identical mark, you may find it costly and difficult to prove that you were the first user of it.

Proposals to introduce a European Community trade mark (and also, probably a Community service mark) are well advanced. This would mean that a single application would be enough to secure protection in the whole of the Community.

registered designs

Registering the design of some invention, or other object, is a method of protecting not the way in which it functions (which should be protected by a patent), but the way it looks: its appearance, its appeal to the eye. This protection is in addition to any copyright that may exist and does not detract from it.

The designer applies to the Design Registry at the Patent Office, furnishing a representation, or specimen, or photographs of the design. The design is examined to see whether it is new or original and complies with other requirements of the Registered Designs Acts. If it does, a certificate of registration is issued, which gives the proprietor the sole right to manufacture, sell or use in business, articles which look identical (or very similar) to the design submitted for registration. The fee depends on the nature of the article and design – from £12 to £81, at present. This protection lasts for 5 years in the first instance, and can be renewed for two further periods of 5 years (current fees £99 and £146).

To be accepted as new, a design must not have been disclosed to the public in the UK in any way.

The protection is intended to apply to industrial designs, that is, only the appearance of articles manufactured in quantity. Its scope does not cover such features as shape or configurations that are strictly part of the function of the article. This means that the appearance of many mechanical components and articles whose shape is determined solely by the need to do the job, and not by its appeal to the eye, cannot be protected as a registered design. (Such articles may however be protected by copyright if an original drawing exists.)

A pamphlet entitled *Protection of Industrial Designs*, which also lists fees, and the necessary forms are available free of charge from the Design Registry at the Patent Office.

protection abroad

Designs may also be registered in other countries. Under the International Convention for the Protection of Industrial Property, anyone who registers a design in the UK has six months from the date of application in which to apply for registration in other countries, and during that period his priority over later applicants is maintained.

copyright

The law of copyright forbids the unauthorised reproduction of an artist's or craftsman's work.

It was originally brought in to protect authors' rights in their written work, and was later extended to other media, such as films, records and the graphic arts. Engineering drawings are also protected. What is most important, copyright is infringed if such drawings are copied in three dimensions, that is, if they are reproduced in the form of objects.

Copyright is automatic and no registration is required, but the author or draughtsman needs to be able to prove authorship: he should be able to show his original drawing and the rough drawings it was based on. All of these should have been signed, dated, and the signature witnessed; preferably they should be marked with the international copyright symbol, 'c' inside a circle © accompanied by the year of first publication and the copyright owner's name.

Copyright protection lasts for the author's/designer's lifetime, and for 50 years after his death. One important exception to this: where a work is capable of being a registered design, then the copyright is limited to 15 years from the date when an article based on the design is first manufactured in quantity.

There is sometimes a useful overlap between the protection afforded by copyright, and the monopoly right conferred by patent. For instance, any designs, drawings or models of a patented invention would be subject to copyright.

There is an essential difference between the two kinds of protection: to establish infringement of copyright, you have to prove that your work was copied, whether directly or indirectly.

To establish the infringement of a patent, there is no need to prove copying; all depends on the wording of the patent by which the monopoly right was granted.

getting help
If you need to take out a patent or register a trade or service mark or a design, you will be well advised to seek the help of a patent agent, because the legislation relating to all this is complex. Londoners can use the London Enterprise Agency's free innovations service for advice on protecting new ideas, and similar agencies may be able to offer help in other areas of the country.

▲ If you want to thread your own way through the maze, the Science Reference Information Service, 25 Southampton Buildings, Chancery Lane, London WC2A 1AY (telephone: 01-636 1544), comprises a vast and comprehensive library relating to inventions, patents, trade marks and so on. It is open to the public.

The Patent Office operates an 'awareness programme', based on a series of seminars and lectures, which are tailored to the requirements of particular clients or groups. For further information, ring the Patent Office at 01-829 6512.

BEING A RETAILER

Every High Street is the same – every High Street is different: paradoxically, both statements are true. From town to town, the first impression is of sameness, with the familiar chain stores and multiples, Boots, W. H. Smith, Sainsbury's and many others in various combinations in every shopping centre of any size. But if you look more closely, you will notice among the famous fascias many belonging to the smaller businesses, with just the one shop, or perhaps one or two branches. And in villages and suburban shopping parades the individual businesses will be in the majority; some old-established, others recently started, all determined to keep their end up.

These are not easy times for retail businesses: the shopkeepers are fighting the huge organisations for a share of the customers' dwindling spending power, and are using considerable ingenuity in doing so.

The multiples, with their enormous resources, vast floor space and the ability to command the whole output of a factory, have an undoubted advantage in cutting prices and offering a large variety of lines. The smaller shops that do not evolve and adapt to meet this challenge are fighting tanks with bows and arrows.

Some practise guerrilla warfare, turning their small size to advantage in offering kinds of service that are not worth the big organisations' while: opening very early or staying open very late; delivering to customers' houses; and various others. The small shop's strongest weapon is the element of service which is the one thing the giants cannot match. Many people prefer to spend their money where vegetables and groceries will be delivered, a dress altered to fit exactly, do-it-yourself tools sold with some expert advice.

The small shop can sell goods in small quantities: one slice of ham, half a yard of elastic, six screws; in the big stores, such items are prepacked, giving the customer little control over quantity.

Such a service is especially valuable to elderly people whose needs are modest, as are their means. Still, if a shop attracts all the pensioner trade, it should not complain.

That the village shop, has a social as well as a commercial value is widely recognised, and if you hope to join the ranks of those who are trying to keep the village shop alive, get in touch with CoSIRA which has set up an advice service particularly for the benefit of the rural shopkeeper.

Service means labour, and labour is expensive, even though it is – unfortunately for many – no longer so scarce as it used to be. Consider ways of turning this melancholy situation to advantage, perhaps by employing school-leavers or taking on part-timers.

You score if you can harness your whole family into a team, perhaps – if yours is a shop that is allowed to – opening seven days a week (usually only possible if the shop is staffed by the owner's family).

having what it takes

Most people have idyllic childhood memories of playing shop: reality is quite a bit different.

It helps to be an early riser, especially in the food trade, such as a greengrocer who has to go to his wholesalers in the early hours, and be back in time to open the shop. Or there may be early morning deliveries to attend to, as in the case of a newsagent. You may not get to bed very early either, because accounts, stock control, VAT, ordering, dealing with credit card business may all have to be dealt with in the evening.

The advice that you should acquire some working experience before setting up on your own applies doubly to shopkeeping, not only in order to learn some of the mechanics of the trade but to find out if you are temperamentally suited to it.

If your customers become irate, you will hear about it pretty soon. But no matter how you feel, you will have to appear unfailingly cheerful, patient, polite, and helpful even when customers offer a good deal of provocation. An offended customer is unlikely to return.

opening hours

The trading hours of shops are still regulated by the Shops Act 1950, the gist of which is that shops may open at whatever time they like, but must close by 8pm on weekdays, 9pm on one week night (late shopping night); in many places this is friday. Shops may open on sundays to sell a limited range of goods: newspapers, magazines, cigarettes, tobacco, sweets, milk, fresh vegetables, cooked food and various other items, usually of a perishable nature, or related to entertainment (guide books, postcards) or emergencies (medicines, surgical appliances).

Shops must close by 1pm one day a week (not necessarily all on the same one) unless the majority of the shopkeepers in the district petition for this regulation to be relaxed. Some shops are exempt from the early closing rule: the criteria are roughly the same as for sunday opening.

There are relaxations for shops in holiday areas, which may stay open on some sundays to sell holiday goods (e.g., camera film, fishing rods). Some shops owned by Jews which close on saturdays may open on sundays.

You will probably have noticed the law about shop hours being broken right and left. Many local authorities take a relaxed attitude to this, especially when the shop is staffed by the members of the owner's family. It is as well to find out your own local authority's stand, if you plan to stay open outside the prescribed hours. The parliamentary defeat in April 1986 of the hoped-for revision of the Shops Act may cause some previously tolerant local authorities to insist on strict observance of the law.

premises for a retail business

There is one common factor shared by almost all retail businesses: the need for a street frontage. Generally this means that the shopkeeper must find ready-built premises in a shopping centre (though if it is a new development, he may be the first occupier).

He needs to choose the right shop in the right location in the right district, and adapt it to his own needs.

choosing the district

It is doubtful whether anybody chooses an area in which to trade completely at random. You, too, will probably have reasons of your own for wishing to open a shop in one part of town rather than another.

By all means use your inclination as a starting point, but keep an open mind: if your investigations show that the preferred district is a no-hoper, look elsewhere.

Find out, preferably by personal investigation over a period of time, whether the area is prosperous or declining. Try to find out what the unemployment rate is: closed-down factories are an ominous sign, if there is an industrial area near by. Note 'For Sale' boards on private houses – if there are many, and they remain for a long time, there may be more people moving away from the area – or trying to – than are coming in. If there are many High Street shops for sale or rent, you will not have any trouble finding one, but you may not do much good there.

Look what other shopping centres there are near by. It may be that the more prosperous residents, the ones with cars, are accustomed to take their business farther away, perhaps to some big, new shopping complex, so that you would have to make do with the shoppers who cannot manage or afford the journey.

Do people come to work in the district? Look for offices, schools, colleges, industrial estates: people who have to shop in their lunch hour seldom go far afield. On the other hand, if you mostly sell to people who commute in, you may be twiddling your thumbs on saturdays, which elsewhere are the best shopping days.

Where there are any other reasons why people should come into the district – a swimming pool, a central library, council offices, a museum or art gallery – all these can bring in potential customers from other districts. If there is a railway station or bus terminus near by, the users may have to pass along the shopping street: good for business.

choosing the location

For a shop, nothing is more important than location: it must be where the customers are. For most, the more prominent the location, the better, because although much of the custom may come from regulars, a good deal comes from passers-by, who are lured to come in on impulse.

A small shop in a small suburban shopping parade probably enjoys little passing trade and may have a captive clientele of local residents, particularly the mothers of young families and the elderly. By staying open later than the High Street shops, it may attract working wives and people who have simply run out of something. If this is the sort of shop you want, finding premises will be largely a question of locating a vacant property. But be careful about competition: there may not be enough trade for two butchers or two hardware merchants.

In a High Street shopping centre, the presence of a competing business may not necessarily be a disadvantage; it can even be a good thing, up to a point.

Where there are several shops of the same kind in a shopping district, it encourages people to travel there; customers like the prospect of choice, an alternative source near by: that source could be your shop. For some kinds of shop, competition is a positive factor: bookshops and shoe shops, for instance. Book-buyers like to drift from shop to shop, browsing: a shoe customer will prefer to know that if the shoes she or he wants are not available in one shop, there is another shoe shop near by. Estate agents, too, gain a collective benefit from being closely associated with each other – people tend to visit a number of agencies, so there is no harm in making it easy for them.

A specialist shop, such as a builder's merchant, or a musical instrument shop, whose custom hardly depends on passing trade, may do well enough in a side street: it will attract specialist customers by becoming known in the trade.

Every shopping street has its 'dead end', where the trade is slower and the shops are less prosperous and change hands more often. It is important to identify and shun this unlucky location (probably marked by a rash of For Sale and To Let boards).

Even in the 'live' part of the street, some locations can be better than others. If you are taking over a going concern, you have, obviously, less choice. But if you are buying or, more probably renting, vacant property to convert to your own use, give preference to one sited where people have to pause: next to a pedestrian crossing, a bus stop, near a parking place.

buying a going concern

If you decide to take over a shop which is at present trading, the first thing you will want to find out is the owner's reasons for selling. They may be genuinely personal – such as ill health, or retirement. Or they may be strategic: perhaps the owner has heard rumours of a huge new supermarket to be built nearby, or of a large local factory closing down, and is getting out while the going is good. Find out, if necessary by questions to the planning authorities, what new developments are planned in the area. A new main road bisecting a shopping district can halve its trade. Designating roads as one-way can be almost equally bad for trade, as it discourages some traffic from entering the area. A new hypermarket or shopping precinct could be fatal.

Or perhaps the present owner simply has not been able to make a success of the business, in which case the question is – can you? You should not only scrutinise the shop's accounts, but if possible also observe the proprietor at work. The reason for his poor financial performance may be idleness, incompetence, understocking or overstocking, understaffing or overstaffing, poor choice of goods or of opening hours. Perhaps it is the location that is at fault, and no shop in that line of business could succeed there.

There are other considerations: if the fixtures and fittings are not to your liking, how much will it cost to refit the shop? There may be no choice whether to buy or rent the premises. When renting, which is more common, you must know how long the lease has to run, whether it is renewable and on what terms. In a repairing lease, the consequent dilapidation liability must be allowed for in financial planning.

There is also the problem of what the goodwill is worth. A shop which is doing poorly cannot claim much of that, but even if it is doing well you cannot be sure that the customers are regulars who will transfer their custom to you.

You will, of course, have the property valued by a professional valuer and its leases and accounts throughly inspected, before coming to a decision.

starting a new business
You may be looking for an empty property in order to start a completely new shop. Where such a property is brand-new, in a newly built development, it may be difficult to assess your potential custom. But you should at least inspect the district; ideally, the development should include new housing or be near a residential area or a commuter area.

If you are thinking of taking over empty premises previously used as a shop, find out why the previous owner closed down: perhaps this is one of those 'dead' sites where no business ever succeeds.

You will have to clear any change of use with the local authority's planning department. But if you intend to carry on a business of a similar character to the previous one, there is likely to be no problem. Most retail businesses are considered as interchangeable, and you can freely convert from one kind to another without permission. However, if you carry out any structural alterations to the building, your plans must be approved in the usual way.

You should consult your fire prevention officer for your own good, even if you think you do not come under any regulations. Some kinds of businesses, such as garages, which have special fire hazards, have their own regulations.

accepting credit cards
If your goods carry a profit margin reasonably in excess of the credit card companies' commission (at present around 4 to 5 per cent), you may decide to try to attract more customers by becoming what is called a credit card agent.

When you have signed an agreement with the credit card company, you will be supplied with vouchers, a printer, and instructions how to use them. You may be given an envelope in which to send or hand the vouchers to the bank, or you can hand them over to a cashier at the bank, as you would cash or cheques. Your account is immediately credited with the full amount on the slips, and the percentage due to the credit card company is direct-debited from your account to theirs. You receive a regular statement from the credit card company showing all the transactions, and the service charge or commission deducted.

Each retail outlet has a 'floor limit' which is the amount above which the retailer must telephone the credit card company for authorisation.

But credit card trading is not appropriate to some forms of retail trade, such as food shops or others where the margin of profit is low, because of the credit card company's service charge or commission. You must not charge the customers differently according to whether they pay by credit card or not, in order to recoup yourself for the commission.

accepting luncheon vouchers

If you sell pre-prepared food in any form, from full restaurant meals to snacks and sandwiches, and you want to accept Luncheon Vouchers, you have to make sure that they are used for food only. The address of Luncheon Vouchers Limited is 50 Vauxhall Bridge Road, London SW1V 2RS (telephone: 01-834 6666). They will send you full details and display signs for your windows.

You have to count the vouchers and take them or send them to the company for reimbursement. There is a service charge on the redemption of the vouchers; this varies from 0.8% to 1.2%, depending on the volume. In exchange, Luncheon Vouchers guarantee payment in nine days, and also pay for the postage and insurance of the parcel in transit.

buying stocks

This is the heart of the matter for any shopkeeper: he invests a large proportion of his capital in his stock, and must buy it wisely.

how much to stock

Some products deteriorate rapidly (flowers, bread, green-groceries); others do not spoil with keeping, but go out of fashion (clothes, shoes). Even when they neither spoil nor date (most hardware), if nobody buys them, they bring in no profit with which to buy new stock, and take up the space needed for this stock. So, in every case, a rapid turnover of stock is desirable. Stock unsold is cash tied up or lost.

Do not be tempted to over-stock, perhaps by an attractive quantity discount, nor to diversify too much.

The ideal is to buy only what your customers want, and to buy no more of it than you are able to sell.

You could buy through a symbol group, if you belong to one; or from a wholesaler; or from a cash-and-carry warehouse (a kind of retailers' supermarket); or directly from a manufacturer. They are not mutually exclusive. You might think that your orders are unlikely to be large enough to qualify for the quantity discounts which the manufacturer makes available to buying organisations and wholesalers, but do not dismiss the idea of buying direct from manufacturers.

symbol groups

Some shopkeepers, particularly in the grocery trade, take on the big battalions with their own weapons by joining a voluntary symbol group which is a retailers' buying organisation (such as VG, Spar, Mace, Wavy Line) in order to secure the large discounts that manufacturers offer to bulk-buyers.

The retailer agrees to take a certain amount of goods each week from the designated wholesaler for his area and receives better terms than he would get on his own, and possibly other advantages such as a fascia with the group's symbol and the shop's name, help with the layout and fixtures. In some cases, start-up help is given: the wholesaler may give the newcomer help in finding a shop and finance for it.

Details of the relevant head offices and wholesalers are listed in the Grocer Marketing Directory available from the publishers, ▲ William Reed Ltd, 5–7 Southwark Street London SE1 1RQ (telephone: 01-407 6981), price £8 (or try your reference library). The trade press, mainly grocery, but also, for example, hardware, also carries such information. The applicant shopkeeper must offer some evidence of financial security, such as a bank reference. If he is already in business, the wholesaler will inspect the premises to see that they are in line with the organisation's requirements.

If there are other shops belonging to the particular symbol group in the neighbourhood, the wholesaler may refuse to take on another.

Members of the group must undertake to purchase more than a specific amount regularly, and to stock a certain number of the organisation's own-brand products, but are free to buy goods from agencies other than the designated wholesaler.

buying direct or from wholesalers?
When you first open your shop, if you are in a price-competitive field, it is important to try to open with a bang, not a whimper. Your opening offers should be good, and as the initial stocking of the shop is likely to be your largest single stockbuying for a long time, you may qualify for a quantity discount on this order. This is also the time to establish contact with the representatives of the major firms (probably four to eight) whose products are likely to account for a large part of your turnover. The manufacturers' representatives will have a good idea of what are competitive retail prices for the particular products, and may help you to reach them by means of promotional allowances, that are extra discounts, or by providing redeemable 'money off' coupons for customers.

Obviously, you must check that you are not overlooking other sources of supplies that are cheaper, by joining a symbol group and finding a good cash-and-carry source.

Plan your opening carefully: there is no second chance to make a good first impression. Choose about twenty top selling lines and be prepared for very low profit margins on these. They can be from a mixture of sources; choose the best items from each.

When stocking your shop initially, you may be able to negotiate extended credit from your supplier, perhaps no payment for two months, then one-sixth of your opening order to be paid for over the following six months.

An advantage of dealing direct with the manufacturer is that if there are damages, the reps have facilities for exchange or credit which a symbol group or cash-and-carry store may not afford to you. A keen rep can use these facilities to give the retailer a little extra discount on his purchases. You should be aware that damages eat into profit margins just as outdated stock does.

It is possible that manufacturers are less likely to run out of stock than a buying group – and lost sales lead to lost customers. But an advantage of indirect buying, if you stock many items, is cutting down on the time it takes to accept and check deliveries: much of your stock will arrive on one van, or, in the case of a cash-and-carry, be collected by you from one address. There will also be a considerable saving in paperwork.

what to stock?
There is, of course, no single answer to the question of which products and lines you ought to stock. It is partly common sense, partly flair, and partly experience – so here, too, it helps to have worked in the trade.

Customers hardly ever give prior notice of their wants, but expect to find what they want when they want it. And if it is not there in your shop, they go somewhere else, rather than wait for it to be ordered. So the shopkeeper must keep on his toes, trying not to run out of anything, especially the most popular lines.

This demands keeping proper records and a constant check on what goes out, plus efficient and far-sighted reordering, which takes account of the fact that manufacturers do not always meet delivery dates, and that wholesalers have been known to run out of some products. A computer with the appropriate software can help in stock control (and at the same time indicate the profitability of various types of stock).

You must store your stock in such a way that it deteriorates as little as possible and does not acquire that grubby, shopworn look which is so off-putting to customers.

You must rotate it, making sure that articles bought at the earliest period are put on sale first. Some food products are marked with 'sell by' dates, or shelf-life limits, and become unsaleable, once these dates are passed.

Goods which have failed to sell or have passed the peak of saleability should be marked down in price, or thrown away, if perishable. Apart from taking up space fruitlessly, they create a bad impression. You might hold a seasonal sale or sell off unwanted stock week by week, or even day by day, depending on the type of goods.

display

When you think of shops, you think of windows, their distinguishing feature. No other kind of business depends so much on visual display to attract customers.

What is essential is that the display should appear fresh, uncluttered and up-to-date: not dusty, crowded and superannuated. The window should be well-lit, as eye catching as possible, and changed fairly often. If there is any item that you want to promote specially, it should have pride of place.

Prices should be clearly marked, whenever possible. Leaving off price tickets does not encourage people to come inside to ask the price: it is more likely to make them suspicious and put them off.

If you decide to make your shop self-service, the goods must be easily accessible and each article marked with its price. And you must make sure that the checking-out will not create a bottleneck.

When you acquire a shop, the previous owner's fixtures and fittings may suit your purpose exactly, but it is more probable that you will want to make some changes, if only by redecorating. If you are changing the nature of the shop's trade, you will want to start from scratch.

Plan this carefully beforehand, making a list of your requirements and a provisional sketch of the layout; then get estimates from several firms of specialist shopfitters, choosing the one that offers the best value for money. Visit any relevant trade exhibitions such as Shopex which is held every June at Olympia, London, and concentrates on shopfitting, self-service and display equipment. Use your buying group facilities and choose the best that you can afford. Fittings have to last a long time and penny-pinching at the initial state might prove expensive later.

coping with theft

A shopkeeper can be stolen from in various ways: by having his shop broken into, by pilferers on his own staff, by shoplifters (these last two are politely known as 'shrinkage').

shopbreaking

You cannot make your shop burglar-proof, but you can make it harder to burgle. Before you start trading, consult the crime prevention officer at your local police station, and perhaps get a good security firm to inspect the premises and install all necessary devices: locks and/or bolts on all doors and windows (not forgetting the basement and the attic); burglar alarms, not so sensitive that they go off all the time; and anything else that seems sensible. But make sure that what you do does not conflict with the fire prevention regulations.

Other precautions include great attention to locking up; every key accounted for at all times; a light left on all night. Do not leave money in the till overnight; leave the till open at night – a thief would open it anyway, causing unnecessary damage (most insurance companies insist on this). Do not have large sums of money in the shop at any time. Send someone to the bank with it. After banking hours, use the night safe.

You should have adequate insurance from the beginning of trading. If you do happen to be burgled, good stock control will pay off, as you will find it easier to list what has been stolen, which will help in getting your claim settled more promptly.

pilferage by staff

This can be anything from a hand in the till to stealing from stock. By and large, it is the bigger firms' problem: supermarkets have the highest rate of shrinkage. The small shop run by the owner and his family needs less internal protection. But there should be rules about employees' own purchases from the shop.

Although it is difficult to know who is trustworthy, you should be as discriminating as possible about whom you employ. Demand, and take up, references. It is a nerve racking business and not likely to improve relations with staff, having to practise eternal vigilance, constantly checking the deliveries, the stock, the till. Experience will teach you what precautions are necessary.

shoplifting

This is more of a problem if the shop has a self-service layout, or if the goods are displayed on stands or racks (as in many clothes shops). You will hardly be able to afford to employ a shop detective, but it might be worth while to consider renting a closed-circuit TV system; you will get back some of the cost in tax relief. Often the presence itself of such a system is a deterrent. Place the monitor screen so that it can also be seen by customers.

Strategically placed mirrors, perhaps convex ones, can help a lot, at modest cost. The shop itself should be well lit, with no murky corners, and shelves or racks of goods should have full light on them.

Expensive pocketable items, such as calculators, for example, can be chained to the stands: perhaps electrically connected so that a buzzer sounds if the chain is removed.

Advice on these and other anti-theft devices can be sought from a security firm specialising in shop protection.

Vigilence is essential, but however suspiciously a customer may be behaving, do not challenge him until he has removed an article from the premises. Only if theft has taken place, and you have good grounds of suspecting who did it, can you make a citizen's arrest of a shoplifter. If you 'arrest' someone and then he or she is acquitted, so that no theft has been proved to have taken place, the arrest would be unlawful and you could be made to pay heavy damages.

'dud' cheques

When you accept a cheque, there is always a possibility that it may bounce, unless you insist on the production of a cheque card, and write its number down on the back of the cheque. This guarantees payment if you took the cheque in good faith, and you can insist on the bank paying up, to a set limit (at present £50) even if the chequebook and card should turn out to have been stolen, or if the customer's account is empty. Some shops are willing to take two or three cheques for single purchases costing over the limit, but this invalidates the bank's guarantee of the cheque card, and possibly none of the part-payment cheques would be honoured.

Do not accept any other identification, such as a driving licence, since it does not guarantee the owner's solvency. Do not accept cheques for more than the current £50 limit without checking with the customer's bank, or holding up delivery of the goods until the cheque has been cleared.

credit card fraud

The holders of credit cards such as Barclaycard, Access, American Express, Diners Club, are supposed to notify the issuing organisation as soon as they discover a card to have been lost or stolen. If you accepted a stolen card in good faith, however, the issuing organisation will pay you the money. The credit card company may send details of stolen cards to shops which are likely to be at risk, with instructions not to accept those cards. But it is difficult for a shop to check back every single card that is offered.

Card companies pay rewards for lost or stolen cards which are picked up by shops, but may refuse to accept transactions resulting from the use of cards which have been listed as stolen.

learning the law

The shopkeeper must comply with a number of laws, both civil (such as the Sale of Goods Act 1979, the Unfair Contract Terms Act 1977 and the Supply of Goods and Services Act 1982) and criminal (such as the Trade Descriptions Act 1968, the Fair Trading Act 1973 and the Price Marking (Bargain Offers) Order 1979). The New Consumer Protection Act will soon replace the provisions of the 1979 order and Section 11 of the 1968 Act on prices.

Other relevant criminal legislation includes the Food Act 1984 and the Weights and Measures Act 1985: these form a series of special rules and regulations which apply to food.

All these pieces of legislation aim at enforcing the principles of fair trading, and the intending shopkeeper should make himself thoroughly familiar with them. Advice can be sought from each local trading standards department.

▲ The Consumers' Association's advisory services department, 14 Buckingham Street, London WC2N 6DS (telephone: 01-839 1222) runs training courses for retailers on the subject of how the law affects them, with special reference to sales and credit legislation.

Sale of Goods Act 1979

The sale of goods legislation has guided the relationship between the seller and the buyer for nearly a century. The Sale of Goods Act 1893 was the first piece of legislation actually to set down in writing the legal position existing between the seller and the buyer in a contract for the sale of goods, and now, the Sale of Goods Act 1979 still provides the foundation of the present law relating to the sale of goods. The 1979 Act gives protection to each buyer by implying certain rights or terms (known as conditions) into every contract for the sale of goods. The most important of these are that:

○ the goods correspond with the description applied to them – whether orally, or on the container, packaging, wrapping, labelling or other advertising;

○ the goods are of merchantable quality – that is, that they work properly, are in a satisfactory state, and are suitable for the ordinary, everyday purpose for which goods of that kind are usually bought. The buyer must be given value for the money he has paid for them;

○ the goods are fit for the particular purpose – that is, not only must they work properly and be well-made, but fit for the particular purpose that the buyer wants them for, whether that is an ordinary, everyday purpose or an extraordinary or unusual one. For example, a carpet may be of merchantable quality but quite unsuitable for use in a specific location; but when the shopkeeper sells it to meet a specific requirement, it must be reasonably fit for the purpose specified. If the shopkeeper does not know whether or not the commodity will meet the customer's specific needs, he should make it clear that he does not know and therefore cannot advise the buyer.

Second-hand, reduced, and shop-soiled goods are all protected by the requirement of 'merchantable quality'. Such goods may be imperfect, but the buyer is entitled to fair value for the money he has paid for them.

The shopkeeper, too, is afforded some measure of protection, and the buyer has no right to claim that unmerchantable goods have been sold to him where:

○ the shopkeeper specifically drew the buyer's attention to the faults or defects being complained about before the sale was made, *or*

○ the buyer examined the goods before the sale was made and should have seen the faults or defects being complained about for himself.

Breach of any of these conditions, or major contract terms, amounts to a breach of contract, and it is for the shopkeeper to put the matter right between his customer and himself. The customer is entitled to reject the goods, to reclaim the purchase price in full and to claim compensation for any loss or damage that has happened as a direct result of the contract being broken, such as the cost of re-papering and painting where a faulty cooker has exploded causing damage to the kitchen walls and ceiling. Afterwards, the shopkeeper can make a similar claim against his own supplier or the manufacturer, being now himself the aggrieved party.

The Limitation Act 1980 allows the buyer to bring a court action for breach of contract against the shopkeeper at any time up to six years from the date when the cause of action first arises (usually, the date of purchase). The same time limit covers actions between the shopkeeper and his supplier for breach of contract.

Where there is nothing wrong with a product as regards description, quality or fitness, and the buyer simply changes his mind about it, there is no legal obligation on the part of the shopkeeper to give a refund, or even an exchange. If he does so, it is purely a gesture of goodwill. Similarly, the mere recipient of a gift, where something was bought for another person, is outside the scope of the contract of sale, being neither the seller nor the buyer. He also is not entitled to a refund, and if the shopkeeper decides to give him one, or to exchange, this is done as a gesture of goodwill, and not because of any legal liability on the shopkeeper's part.

Unfair Contracts Terms Act 1977

The Unfair Contract Terms Act is concerned, in part, with restricting or preventing the shopkeeper from avoiding his liability towards a customer. He must not incorporate into the contract any so-called 'exclusion clause' which would restrict his responsibility and liability for any breach of legal duty towards the customer.

This includes trying to get out of accepting liability for loss or damage of articles entrusted to you for servicing, or trying to exclude liability for the late delivery of goods that you had promised by a certain time.

The Act, however, allows an exclusion clause in dealings between the shopkeeper and the manufacturer, but only where that clause is a reasonable one. The Act itself sets out guidelines as to the test of reasonableness to be applied, and if a manufacturer wishes to rely on any particular exclusion clause, the burden of proof will be placed on him to show that the clause is fair and reasonable in the circumstances.

Supply of Goods and Services Act 1982
The Supply of Goods and Services Act brings into statute law the various sorts of protection which the consumer has previously enjoyed under common law. Goods supplied as part of a service, on hire, or in part exchange, must fulfil the same conditions (such as being of merchantable quality, fit for the purpose, conforming to description) as the Sale of Goods Act lays down for goods that are being sold.

The Act also sets out clearly that the customer should be able to expect any service he pays for to be carried out with reasonable care and skill, within a reasonable time and (unless a fixed price has already been agreed between the parties) at a reasonable price.

Where the service takes the form of a particular skill – such as, for example, a hairdresser providing a 'cut and blow-dry' – the reasonable standard of care and skill required would be that expected of a reasonably competent member of the hairdressing profession. The work done in providing the service must have been authorised by the customer, and the retailer cannot expect payment for work done over and above what had been agreed between the customer and himself.

worth getting and reading
A free booklet giving an outline of the basic consumer rights can
▲ be obtained from the Office of Fair Trading, Room 310c, Field House, 15-25 Bream's Buildings, London EC4A 1PR (telephone: 01-242 2858). This booklet comes in three editions: *How to put things right* (for England and Wales); *Dear shopper in Scotland*; and *Dear shopper in Northern Ireland*.

Although nominally addressed to shoppers, the booklet contains much useful information for traders, about their various obligations to customers. A summary leaflet, *Shops and shoppers*, is also produced by the OFT, and is available in quantity, for use as a point-of-sale giveaway.

▲ *Croner's Reference Book for Self-employed and Smaller Business*, 173 Kingston Road, New Malden, Surrey KT3 3SS (telephone: 01-942 8966) includes explanatory notes on selected Acts of Parliament. It has a loose-leaf format, and the price, £39.90, includes the first year's updating service, in the form of replacement pages: in subsequent years, this costs £23.60 a year.

Law for Retailers by Jennifer Brave, published by Sweet & Maxwell (£7.95), sets out the key areas of law as they apply to retailers, and contains details of fresh legislation of direct relevance to retailers, including sale of goods, trade descriptions, bargain offers, credit, consumer safety, theft and related offences, and negligence and product liability.

receipts

The practice of giving the customer a written receipt as proof of purchase is a fundamental one to the retail business, but at common law there is no legal obligation on the part of the retailer to give a receipt, nor for the customer to produce one. The absence of a written receipt does not necessarily mean that the goods have not been paid for – the receipt could have been lost, or the shopkeeper may have omitted to give one in the first place. The law allows the shopper to prove his purchase not only by written proof (such as a till receipt or the customer portion of a credit card voucher) but also verbally (by 'parole evidence' – simply stating that he bought the items from that retailer).

That is why the law forbids the shopkeeper to put up notices and display signs, or their equivalent, saying such things as: "Refunds cannot be given in the absence of a written receipt" which imply to the customer that complaints will be dealt with only on written proof of purchase. Statements like this are illegal, and the shopkeeper cannot rely on them.

Fair Trading Act 1973

The criminal law imposes further limits or restrictions on the shopkeeper relating to statements he may wish to make to his customer, by virtue of the Consumer Transactions (Restrictions on Statements) Orders 1976 and 1978. These also apply to the manufacturer of goods, and have their origin in the Fair Trading Act 1973.

The Orders make it a criminal offence for a shopkeeper or a manufacturer to 'cut out' the statutory rights – as to merchantable quality, fitness for the particular purpose, and conforming to description – afforded to the customer by the Sale of Goods Act 1979, whether by means of a display notice, a wrapper, label, packaging, advertisement, or the goods themselves.

For this reason, each of the following statements is illegal and you can be prosecuted in respect of each of them: 'no money refunded', 'for hygiene purposes, goods not exchanged or money refunded', 'sale goods not exchanged nor money refunded',and 'credit notes only for faulty goods'.

Breach of the Orders is a criminal offence, which is punishable by fine, imprisonment or both. Enforcement in each locality is carried out by the trading standards or consumer protection department.

Trade Descriptions Acts 1968 and 1972

The law of trade descriptions is of tremendous importance. Breach of it is a criminal offence, punishable by fine, imprisonment or both. Enforcement is the duty of the local trading standards or consumer protection department, whose duly authorised officers have power to make test purchases, to enter premises and inspect and seize goods and documents for the purpose of determining whether or not the law is being complied with. Respect should be shown for their office, which, incidentally, dates as far back as Magna Carta. Any person who wilfully obstructs a trading standards officer, or who wilfully fails to comply with a valid request by such an officer, or who without reasonable cause fails to give any other assistance asked for, commits the offence of obstruction.

Trading standards officers will also be pleased to provide guidance and advice, should you wish to consult them.

The 1968 Act creates a basic set of criminal offences by generally prohibiting false trade descriptions. It makes it an offence for a shopkeeper to describe goods falsely and to sell, or offer for sale, goods so misdescribed. It applies to all aspects of retailing and includes advertisements, display cards, illustrations, labelling, packaging, brochures, ticketing and statements made verbally.

It covers descriptions as to quality, quantity, size, method or process of manufacture, composition, performance, fitness for purpose, testing, approval by any person, previous history of the goods, place or date of manufacture or processing, and by whom made.

If things go wrong, and proceedings have been taken against the shopkeeper for supplying or offering to supply goods to which a false trade description is applied, he has a defence if he can prove that he did not know, and could not with reasonable diligence have found out, that the goods did not match the description, or that the description had been applied to the goods in question.

The shopkeeper also has a defence in cases where an offence has been committed through mistake or an accident, or through the act or default of another person, or some other cause beyond his (the shopkeeper's) control. He must show that he 'took all reasonable precautions' *and* 'exercised all due diligence' to avoid an offence being committed. In other words, the shopkeeper must have a system in operation to avoid the commission of any offence, and that system must be effective.

Section 11 of the Trade Descriptions Act 1968 contains special rules about price. These remain in force at the time of publication, but they will be repealed and replaced by the new provisions of the Consumer Protection Act and any subsequent Regulations made under it. There will also be practical guidelines available for traders, in the form of a new Code of Practice. Contravention of, or compliance with the Code will tend to establish whether or not a price indication is misleading.

Under Section 11 of the 1968 Act, where you display a price ticket stating, 'Now £4, reduced from £6.50', you must have previously offered the goods in question, or goods of the same description, at the higher price of £6.50 for at least 28 consecutive days in the preceding six months. If this is not the case, you must display what is known as a disclaimer, a notice saying, for example, that the goods were previously offered at a higher price, but were not so offered for a continuous period of at least 28 days in the preceding six months.

The concept of 'disclaimers' will not be part of the new law – the Consumer Protection Act makes no provision for them. It is proposed to extend the 28-day rule from a period of at least 28 continuous days in the last six months to the new provision of at least 28 consecutive days during the previous 12 months. No definite decision has been reached at the time of publication, and you should consult Trading Standards officers on this point when the new law comes into force.

Under Section 11 of the 1968 Act, it is an offence for a shop-keeper to give any false indication that the price of goods is equal to, or less than, a recommended price. Where you sell something at a 'recommended price', this (unless the contrary is expressed) has to be the price generally recommended by the manufacturer as the price for retail supply in the area where the goods are offered. You must be able to substantiate this by a current catalogue or price list.

The Consumer Protection Act will see the creation of a new *general* offence of giving to consumers a misleading price indication about any goods or services, and a second *related* offence to deal with the situation where a price indication, though not misleading at first, subsequently becomes misleading. Recommended prices will, therefore, be caught by the new provisions, as will other matters of price.

The new Consumer Protection Act will also bid farewell to the provisions of the Trade Descriptions Act 1972 on origin marking. Current provisions impede the free trade provisions of the Treaty of Rome between member states of the European Community. Repeal of the 1972 Act will be synchronised with the introduction of a new obligation on origin marking which is aceptable in Community law.

Price Marking (Bargain Offers) Order 1979 as amended

The general effect of the Order is to prohibit prices and charges for consumer goods and services being quoted in a way which claims or implies that the price or charge in question is lower than another price or charge for goods or services of the same description UNLESS the price quotation can be justified by specific exemptions referred to in the Order. These include

– comparison with your own previous higher price,

- comparison with your own proposed higher price,
- comparisons with a price applicable to a specified group or class of people (such as pensioners, for example), and
- comparisons of goods or services, of the same description, sold in different circumstances;

    different condition such as 'seconds' compared to 'first quality';

    different quantity (such as 40p each or 3 for £1); or on specified different terms.

These provisions remain in force at the time of publication. When the 1979 Order is repealed, similar provisions will apply under the Consumer Protection Act and will be set out, either in new Regulations, or in the Code of Practice.

Where a shopkeeper makes a comparison with his own previous price, at least one item must, at some time, have been sold at the higher price. If the higher price quoted was charged at other store premises within that company and not at the shop or store in question, then the other store must be named and identified.

It is not possible to disclaim these requirements. Where such a price comparison is made, the provisions of the Trade Descriptions Act 1968 regarding the 28-day rule, *and* the rules of the Bargain Offers Order just referred to must be satisfied every time.

With the coming into force of the price provisions of the Consumer Protection Act, it will not be necessary to have sold one item at the higher price, but it will still be necessary, in certain circumstances, to name the locations where goods or services have been offered at a higher price.

Certain prohibitions currently exist as to the use of recommended prices, for price comparison purposes, for certain specified categories of merchandise. These prohibitions will still apply under the new law, and are as follows:

○ beds (except campbeds and beds intended primarily for outdoor use) but including mattresses and headboards
○ domestic appliances operated by electricity, gas or other fuel (for example, dishwashers, irons, vacuum cleaners, freezers, grills, hotplates, toasters, hair dryers, etc), including their accessories and attachments

○ consumer electronic goods – designed exclusively or mainly for
  domestic use (for example, radio, TV, hi-fi), including their
  accessories and attachments
○ carpets – including mats, rugs, carpet tiles and carpet underlays
○ furniture – including unassembled furniture and kitchen furniture, but excluding garden furniture and soft furnishings.

As now, the new law will prevent 'worth' and 'value' claims,
such as 'worth £10 – our price £5".

Breach of the 1979 Order is a criminal offence. The defences
available are the same as those provided by the 1968 Act, and
enforcement is by the local trading standards or consumer protection departments.

Consumer Protection Act

In addition to its provisions on pricing and its repeal of origin
marking, the new Act will provide for the introduction of a new
general safety requirement for consumer goods, enforced by criminal sanctions. This requirement applies to anyone who supplies
consumer goods which do not comply with the new safety
standard.

The Act will also introduce into the United Kingdom the
provisions of the European Community Directive on Product
Liability, by bringing into force the concept of strict liability, that
is, liability without fault, for defective products. Liability will be
placed firmly on the shoulders of producers, own branders,
importers, and, in limited circumstances, other suppliers (which
could include retailers). Victims will no longer have the heavy
burden of proving negligence on the part of the manufacturer
when they are injured by defective products.

giving customers credit for goods or services

As a business person, you are perfectly free to give credit to your
customers for goods or services which you have supplied to
them, that is, you can agree to allow them to defer their payment.
Or you may inform the customer that credit will not be available
to him (perhaps because of his low credit rating).

Consumer Credit Act 1974

The Consumer Credit Act 1974 and its subsequent Regulations set down the rules to be followed in dealing with credit – particularly in relation to licensing, credit references, credit cards or tokens, credit advertising and the giving of credit quotations. You need to be aware of all these aspects and of how the law regulates credit agreements between business people and their customers.

The Consumer Credit Act 1974 regulates most of the agreements under which credit is advanced to any person (but not where credit is advanced to a company), regardless of whether the credit agreement is a hire purchase, a conditional sale or a credit agreement in respect of services rendered or goods supplied. It applies whether the person supplying the goods or services provides the credit facility himself or refers his customer to a finance house.

The Act imposes strict rules on advertising credit. It also gives customers the right to require a written quotation, clearly stating the exact terms on which credit is on offer. Although this right is rarely exercised, you need to know about it.

consumer credit business

Any business which provides credit under credit agreements which are regulated by the 1974 Act is called a consumer credit business, for example a shop selling goods on its own credit terms or a finance house which sells goods under hire-purchase agreements.

credit agreements

Before providing credit or hire facilities (such as, for example, renting out television sets or cars) you will need to ask your customer to sign an agreement, setting out his rights and obligations. In many circumstances, he has the right to cancel the agreement: if so, the agreement itself must contain a notice explaining the customer's legal rights. Certain provisions are in force which require various copies of the agreement to be given to the customer. You should be aware of them.

licences

Licensing is an essential part of the legal requirements on credit, and a person who carries on a consumer credit business must first obtain the appropriate credit licence. (If not, he commits a criminal offence). A licence remains valid for 15 years, but it can be varied, suspended or revoked by the Office of Fair Trading where the concept of 'fitness' is put in doubt.

There are 6 categories of credit licence, namely for:

category A – consumer credit business
category B – consumer hire business
category C – credit brokerage
category D – debt adjusting and debt counselling
category E – debt collecting
category F – credit reference agency.

A credit licence is not granted automatically, and each application is carefully vetted by the Office of Fair Trading. The Director General of Fair Trading must be satisfied that the prospective licence holder 'is a fit person to engage in activities covered by the licence' and that 'the name(s) under which he applies to be licensed is (or are) not misleading or otherwise undesirable'. Details of all licence applications are kept in a public register. If an application is turned down (which seldom happens), the shopkeeper can appeal to the Secretary of State for Trade. A right of appeal, on a point of law, can also be made to the courts.

The address to which you should apply for all credit licences is:

▲ The Office of Fair Trading, Consumer Credit Licensing Branch, Government Building, Bromyard Avenue, Acton, London W3 7BB (telephone: 01-743 5566). Licence application forms are also generally available from local authority trading standards departments.

A shopkeeper will need to have a category A licence – which covers those situations where credit is offered to the customer. A shopkeeper, without a licence, who endeavours to enter into any credit agreement will not be able to enforce it against the debtor.

It will, in certain circumstances, be necessary for the shopkeeper to obtain a category C licence where he enters into 'credit brokerage'.

credit brokerage business

Any business which introduces individuals who want credit to other businesses offering such facilities is a 'credit brokerage' business. So, if you do not sell a TV set on credit terms but refer your customer to a company which provides credit facilities, and then sell the TV set to that agency (which, in turn, sells it to the customer on credit), you are operating a credit brokerage business, and as such you must obtain a category C licence.

worth getting and reading

Because consumer credit legislation is very intricate and involves so many regulations and calculations, you should obtain and read very carefully the information booklets, brochures and leaflets
▲ obtainable free of charge from the Office of Fair Trading, Room 310c, Field House, 15-25 Bream's Buildings, London EC4A 1PR (telephone: 01-242 2858). They include: *Credit charges* (how to calculate the total charge for credit and the annual percentage rate of charge); *Licensing* (describing the categories of consumer credit licence); *Advertisements and quotations regulations; Regulated and exempt agreements; Cancellable agreements* and *non-cancellable agreements; Hire agreements; Matters arising during the lifetime of an agreement*.

▲   Amongst the publications of the Consumer Credit Trade Association, Tennyson House, 159–165 Great Portland Street, London W1N 5FD (telephone: 01-636 7564) are *A short guide to the Consumer Credit Act 1974* by C McNeil Greig (£3.50) and by the same author for £2.50 *A short guide to regulations made under the Consumer Credit Act 1974* (how to formulate advertisements for credit and hire; and information about credit quotations, and the total charge for credit), and *A short guide to documents and rebates under the Consumer Credit Act 1974* by P J Patrick (£6.50).

The Consumer Credit Trade Association also provides training to its members to meet requirements connected with all aspects of credit, and publishes detailed information on new legislation. It provides a personal advisory service and supplies the standard documents required under the Consumer Credit Act. The membership fee for a new company is £90 plus £13.50 VAT.

SOME DREAMS EXPLORED

There are some businesses that have an enduring appeal for people hoping to become their own boss: having a bookshop; keeping a pub; being a newsagent. These seem to require no special training, and they bring you into contact with things which are generally associated with pleasure: alcoholic drink, magazines, tobacco, sweets, books.

An employment agency has the appeal of involving dealing with people, something which everybody believes themselves to have a natural flair for.

being a bookseller

Many middleclass, middleaged people have a fantasy of keeping a bookshop because they like the books themselves and the kind of people who buy books. What is more, they imagine that they will start off by selling, secondhand, all those surplus books now on their own shelves at home. The reality is not so promising.

It is not enough to love your stock; you must also know how to sell it. Working for a while in a secondhand bookshop might supply some of the requisite expertise: where to find your stock, how much to pay for it and how to price it so as to make a profit while your customer feels that he is getting a bargain. Some books (for example medical and legal texts) rapidly date and lose their resale value, whereas others (chiefly literary works) may acquire rarity value as they go out of print.

new books

▲ The Booksellers Association of Great Britain and Ireland, 154 Buckingham Palace Road, London SW1W 9TZ (telephone: 01-730 8214) offers advice, information and training. Joining it will make it somewhat easier for you to open accounts with publishers and get stock on credit. The book tokens scheme is open to members only.

The Booksellers Clearing House is a central clearing facility provided by the Association, which enables booksellers to settle a large number of publishers' monthly accounts in one single payment.

Publishers offer the retailer set discount rates, which vary from publisher to publisher and from book to book. Larger orders carry larger discounts, but it is a gamble to buy in a large number of copies on the chance of a potential bestseller. No bookseller can stock more than a fraction of the 400,000 titles in print.

Almost all books published in Britain are price-maintained. Publishers who are members of the Publishers Association sign the 'net book agreement' to the effect that no bookseller will be supplied unless he undertakes to sell books only at the 'net' price fixed by their publisher. Almost all publishers who are not members have a similar agreement. So if you tried to undersell your competitors, you would soon find your sources of supply closed (and you might also find yourself in court). But if you participate in the annual National Book Sale (many booksellers do not), you may sell publishers' overstock at not more than half the published price. You may also sell, as cheaply as you like, any book you have not reordered in the last twelve months.

You may choose to limit your trade to remaindered books, which have no net price: they may be bought from remaindered book merchants who buy up cheaply books in which publishers have no further interest. It is unlikely that you will make your fortune in this way.

keeping a pub

Not all publicans are self-employed, many are managers working for the brewery. To be self-employed, you must either own a free house or, more commonly, rent a public house from a brewery. For this, in the first place write to the brewery of your choice, ask for an interview and give details of yourself and your husband/wife, your experience in licensed trade (if any) and the amount of capital that you have readily available for investment in the pub. The available capital would probably have to be between £10,000 and £25,000 to buy the stock and necessary equipment and give some working capital.

Breweries are selective about tenants, and prefer married couples who will work as a team. You are unlikely to be considered if you are over 55 years old. It is an advantage to have worked in the trade and have had some specific training, apart from general knowledge of retail business. It is not enough to have been a devoted customer. Details of training courses may be obtained from the Brewers' Society, 42 Portman Square, London W1H 0BB (telephone: 01-486 4831).

A pub has to be licensed by the local justices and if you become its tenant you have to apply to be named as the licensee. The application goes to the magistrates who hold licensing sessions at irregular intervals, about 4 times a year, but a protection order can be granted to give temporary authority to carry on the business until a new licence is granted.

If your application to be a tenant is accepted by the brewery, you will be required to enter into a tenancy agreement which, amongst other things, requires you to buy all your beers from the brewery, unless it is unable to supply a type of beer for which you can show demand on the part of your customers. The agreement may also require you to buy your wines, spirits, cider and minerals from the brewer, unless you can show that you are able to get them on more favourable terms elsewhere. All the profits on the sales of liquor and of food remain in your hands.

The work of a publican is hard and requires a capacity for appearing good humoured at all times, while keeping a sharp eye on both customers and staff; short-changing or overcharging customers, or giving friends double measures or cheap drinks is bad for business.

being a newsagent, sweetseller, tobacconist

Running a small shop that sells mainly newspapers is not an easy life, nor outstandingly lucrative. Before you take over an existing shop, apart from the usual checks about the lease and the standing of the business, you must ensure that the wholesaler who is supplying the existing owner will continue to supply newspapers and magazines to you when you take over the shop. There is nothing automatic about this.

There may be a limitation on the numbers of papers that you are allowed to buy on sale or return, and some magazines are supplied on firm sale only. So you might find yourself with unsold stock.

You will need to stay open on every day on which newspapers appear, which is about 360 days of the year. Some newsagents, normally those who do not operate a delivery service, close on sundays, but this makes for lost sales.

You must be up before the lark every day, taking delivery of papers and sorting them and marking them up if you operate delivery rounds. Among your headaches will be sending out bills to tardy customers, explaining to customers why their newspaper or magazine has not arrived – which may be due to industrial action, at the publishers or wholesalers.

If you do home deliveries, you must find schoolchildren to do your rounds and will have to deal with the local education authority inspectors. There are by-laws about employing children to deliver newspapers; the children must be over 13 years old and you must be licensed by the local education authority and adhere to rules such as those about the weight of newspapers they may carry and that the rounds must be finished an hour before school starts. If you employ any adult, minimum wages are laid down by a wages council.

Sweets and tobacco being tempting, pocketable and anonymous, are readily stolen. Selling requires sharp-eyed vigilance both in the stock room and in the shop.

You will have to deal with numerous suppliers offering many lines, so that there will be the need for constant stock checks and reordering. This is where access to a computer might help, especially as the prices you are allowed to charge tend to change with surprising frequency virtually with every Budget.

It is not unusual for a newsagent to work a 90 hour week and do no better than just make a living.

an employment agency

It is important to realise that an employment agency is not easy money, and needs people who are willing to face quite tedious work, have not only drive but also a vast amount of patience, good sales skills and a standard of education that enables them to deal with all types of people. It is important to have, or acquire, proper training in interviewing, backed by a good knowledge of the industry or area in which you intend to operate.

Before starting an agency, consider what type of agency you intend to open – office agency or secretarial and clerical staff plus probably temporary staff in the same categories; or a specialist agency, for example computer staff, nursing staff, accountants, engineers. For specialists, it is important for at least one of the directors or partners to have a good knowledge and understanding of the types of jobs which occur in the particular area of work.

getting the clients
Building up contacts can be achieved by telephone or personal calls, or literature about your business. Calls are likely to be better because the initiative is then yours, not the client's.

A small agency must build up personal contacts and operate on a personal basis but this cannot be rushed, and immediate first-name familiarity on the part of the agency is not always the way in.

It is important always to tell your client the truth about prospective candidates and not to hard-sell the applicant, so that the client will have confidence in your opinions on candidates, and will trust you – which is vitally important. It is no good sending unsuitable applicants to clients in the hope of doing business.

recruiting the applicants
If your premises have a shop front, display the job vacancies for temporary and permanent staff in your windows. Alternatively, and in addition, it is a good idea to advertise permanent job vacancies in a local paper or, for specialist agencies, a national

paper or specialist journals. The wording of the advert should aim to bring in not a quantity, but the right quality, of applicants: the type of candidates who can do the job that is advertised. If you keep a record and analyse your responses from different media, you may learn which are the best to use for a particular type of vacancy.

money matters
If you have temporary workers, you will need a fair amount of capital because you pay the temporary staff straightaway at the end of each week (at an agreed fee per hour, tax and insurance deducted) and although the hourly charge to the client is more (by how much depends on the category of staff) payment from the client may not come in for several weeks.

For permanent staff, you charge an introduction fee of 10–15 per cent of the annual salary. But when you first start an agency, the people whom you place in permanent jobs sometimes do not start their employment immediately, which can result in something like 6 to 8 weeks, or more, passing before you get paid any fees.

formalities
A licence has to be obtained from the Department of Employment before you start. You have to complete an application form with a lot of personal information including the work history of all partners or directors of the proposed agency. You have to display a notice which the Department of Employment lets you have, on the outside of the proposed offices and also put an advertisement with similar wording into the local papers, in case anybody wishes to raise any objection.

Until everything is cleared and a licence granted, it is illegal to carry on any business – so be careful not to sign any binding documents for the proposed offices, such as a lease. An outsider can raise objections to either the newspaper advertisement or the notice outside the proposed office, and if they are sustained by the Department, no licence is then granted.

Running an employment agency involves a great deal of

record-keeping to comply with the Employment Agencies Act. There is probably enough record-keeping, paperwork and book keeping to keep one person fully occupied.

It is also important to have a good broad knowledge of the various statutes and regulations concerning employers and employees.

▲ The Federation of Recruitment and Employment Services Ltd., 10 Belgrave Square, London SW1X 8PH (telephone: 01-235 6616) can give some preliminary advice on running a private recruitment consultancy, and will forward an information pack about the FRES on request: it is the trade association for the private recruitment service, and gives advice on terms of business, documentation, insurance and legal matters, to its members.

▲ The Institute of Employment Consultants, 55 Charterhouse Street, London EC1M 6HA (telephone: 01-251 4559) offers courses in employment consultancy and all aspects of agency work and sets examinations for agency personnel.

AN EXPORTER

A manufacturer who has a product that is competitive on the UK market, but who is looking for another way of increasing his business, may achieve the growth he needs by selling his goods abroad. At the same time he will be spreading his risks, since even if there should be a world recession, it is unlikely that all countries will be equally affected; and being able to manufacture in larger batches may also make him more competitive on the home market.

It is also possible to export without manufacturing, by becoming an export merchant or export agent, and selling abroad goods bought from manufacturers in Britain.

You must pick your markets intelligently, and do some basic research to find out which countries are most likely to want to import what you have to sell, rather than trying to export bacon-flavoured crisps to the middle east; or goods that are prohibited materials in another country according to their national regulations; or goods which do not comply with that country's standard specifications.

Selling abroad carries the same problems as the home trade – plus some others, such as: arranging the packing and shipment of goods to countries perhaps half a world away; complying with a great variety of foreign import regulations; securing payment in a world of shifting currency values and methods of payment. The exporter must be ready to cope with the unforeseen at home (such as a dock strike) and abroad (such as a revolution).

Exporting is not something you can fit into the odd moments you can spare from other concerns. If you plan to manufacture for sale both at home and abroad, either directly or through agents, you will need staff trained to deal with all aspects of exporting.

If your resources do not run to this, you might do better to sell overseas through the established buying offices of overseas companies in the UK, or to entrust your foreign sales to an export merchant, while you concentrate on building up the manufacturing side of your business. When this is on a firm footing, you can gradually build up your own export unit: for instance, by employing part-time, retired export specialists, and by training existing staff. The Institute of Export provides an Export Specialists service, and education and training in exporting.

There is yet another way to export: through buying-houses, or confirming houses, whose function it is to buy for foreign importers of British goods. They send out enquiries to a number of appropriate firms, and then place orders with those which offer the most favourable terms. It is the would-be exporter's job to make himself known to the appropriate buying-houses. You can get a list from the British Overseas Trade Board (BOTB) or the British Export Houses Association, or consult the *Directory of Export Buyers in the UK*; you then make the first approaches yourself, as well as replying to all suitable enquiries.

If you plan to become an export merchant or agent yourself, you will be wise to start with only one or two kinds of goods. Make yourself thoroughly familiar with them, and do not extend your range until you are well established in the trade.

exporting, step by step

Most of the basic steps are the same whether you are dealing with goods manufactured by yourself or by some other firm.

deciding where to export

Your first inkling of a possible market may already have come to you, in the shape of unsolicited enquiries from abroad; or friends in the trade may have mentioned some possible opening. From these, and sources such as the trade press and newspapers, you can pick out one or two possible markets; then you need to do some desk research to find out the most hopeful. For trade figures and general information, go to a good reference library: probably the best is the Statistics and Market Intelligence Library at the ▲ BOTB Headquarters, 1 Victoria Street, London SW1H 0ET. While you are there, you can also visit the product data store which provides a database of product-based and industry-based information about overseas markets. You need to check, among other things, on potential market size, product acceptability, ways of

doing business, technical standards, tariffs, regulations, payment methods and means of shipping. BOTB country desks (at the
same address) can also help you with advice on these matters.

To help small firms trying to sell in western Europe, the BOTB
Exports to Europe Branch publishes *Marketing consumer goods in
Western Europe* and *Country Profiles* for all western European
markets, free of charge. Other useful BOTB publications are: *Help
for exporters; Exporting for the smaller firm;* and *Hints to exporters.*

looking at your product
When you have found one or two markets that look promising,
make sure that your product or service fits the needs of those
markets. A number of organisations can provide you with information free of charge or at subsidised rates: the BOTB, in addition
to its London headquarters, has 10 regional offices throughout
the United Kingdom. Through the BOTB you can obtain commercial information provided by diplomatic service posts.

Other sources are Chambers of Commerce, foreign diplomatic
posts in London, the trade press, and the business sections of the
national press. You should also contact an organisation called
▲ Technical Help to Exporters, Linford Wood, Milton Keynes MK14
6LE (telephone: 0908-220022) for advice on technical requirements
for products in foreign countries: some of the services it offers are
free, others are· charged for. A leaflet giving all the details is
available on request.

developing the market
Amongst the services the BOTB offers is help towards the cost of
overseas market research, and financial support if you join a trade
mission going abroad or participate in an overseas trade fair or
exhibition; it also helps firms to display their products there.

By correspondence and by visits to the markets, you should try
to find channels of distribution; these can vary from direct sales to
individual outlets, to having your own marketing company.
There will probably be companies with established operations
who are prepared to help you, for agreed terms.

The BOTB recommends that you find a good agent in each
market (and will help you with this) and then give him full

back-up support. You will need to develop suitable promotional material; if it is to be in a foreign language, it should be prepared by a native speaker who also has some relevant technical knowledge.

▲ It is important to have a watertight agreement with each overseas agent. The Institute of Export, Export House, 64 Clifton Street, London EC2A 4HB (telephone: 01-247 9812) can advise you.

securing a profit

To ensure a profit from overseas sales, it is important to have reliable channels of distribution. So take professional advice: from a freight forwarder, about the terms on which you should trade; from a broker about insurance; from the international division of your bank, about handling payment. You may also need to secure yourself against credit risks, for example, through the Export Credits Guarantee Department (ECGD), but, if you can, avoid taking such risks when you first start to export.

managing the operation

It is unlikely that anyone will place an order without first receiving a quotation. To save time, send this in the form of a pro-forma invoice – promptly and by airmail.

A pro-forma invoice looks like an ordinary invoice, except for the words 'pro-forma' in the heading. The figures you quote are binding. The invoice should indicate the type and quantity of goods, with details of their prices, the delivery time, the terms of payment (such as letter of credit or sight draft), the currency in which the deal is to be made, the method of packing. It should also state whether the prices quoted are as defined under IMCO (which stands for the United Nations inter-governmental consultative organisation) terms as, for example:

f.a.s. – free alongside ship
   price includes delivery to the docks
f.o.b. – free on board
   price includes delivery on board ship
DCP – cost and freight or carriage (paid to . . .)
   price includes freight charges, but not insurance
   charges, to an agreed port of destination

CIP –   cost, freight or carriage insurance (paid to . . .) price includes both freight and insurance charges to an agreed port of destination.

All the terms should be clearly set out in the quotation or pro-forma invoice, because once the customer has signified his acceptance of this, it becomes a contract binding on both parties. Hence, you should also state how long your offer remains valid. If an order has been confirmed by the customer by telex, it is necessary to get confirmation by letter; pro-forma invoices must also be sent by mail.

dealing with suppliers

Unless you yourself are the manufacturer of the goods, or have them in stock, when you receive an enquiry, you will need to contact the manufacturers or stockists for quotations. You must emphasise that the goods will have to be suitably packed for export. The suppliers' quotations or pro-forma invoices should be with prices quoted f.o.b. or DCP or CIP, as requested.

If a supplier will only quote f.o.b., you must ask for an approximate shipping specification: the number of packages, cartons, cases, etc. that will be needed, the delivery time, their gross and net weights and their shipping measurements. You need this information to estimate the cost of freight, and insurance if required, plus the shipping expenses which the forwarding agents will charge. Your supplier's terms of payment may be cash with order or cash within seven days from receipt of invoice (possibly with a special cash discount); or monthly account (subject to satisfactory trade and bank references); or some other method of payment.

Be very meticulous in comparing your supplier's quotation with the pro-forma invoice you send to your potential customer overseas. Any discrepancies between the supplier's descriptions and the customer's requirements must be sorted out because, once the order is placed, the customer will usually insist on receiving the goods exactly as specified in the pro-forma invoice. Any confusion about whether the prices quoted are f.o.b., DCP or

CIP can play havoc with the calculations of an exporter's expected profit.

Croner's Reference Book for Exporters contains a wealth of information about all aspects of the export trade, with separate entries for every country, giving a summary of its individual import regulations. It is a loose-leaf book, and its price (at present, £49.90) includes a year's updating amendments: the old page is removed and the new one inserted. The annual amendments subscription in subsequent years is (at present) £31.70.

arrangements for shipment

For sending goods by sea or air, you normally need the services of a freight forwarder: he should be a registered trading member of the Institute of Freight Forwarders. An efficient forwarder should advise you on the best method of transportation to your destination, and help you with freight calculations and documentation and with estimating the cost of freight. He can prepare most of the shipping documents, and also arrange full marine insurance on your behalf, if required.

The forwarder can collect the goods from your premises, packing them if necessary; he directs how the goods should be consigned when they are sent to the docks for shipment. If the goods are to be sent f.o.b., he attends to all the shipping details.

When advised that the goods have gone forward to the ship, he will obtain bills of lading. These are detailed receipts for the goods, issued by the shipping company, containing a contract whereby the company undertakes to deliver the goods to a specified port of destination. The bill of lading is the most important part of the transaction: it is the document of title to the goods listed in it.

forwarding freight by air

The procedure is similar to that for shipping, with these differences: the goods are usually collected by the air freight forwarder and taken into his premises prior to being delivered to the airline sheds at the airport. Many forwarders will give quotations on a door to door basis. The document of carriage is called an air waybill, not a bill of lading, and it is not a document of title.

The Institute of Freight Forwarders will supply the names of registered freight forwarders, both for shipping and air freight, free of charge on request, as well as a booklet, *A Brief introduction to freight forwarding*, price 75p.

exporting by post (International Parcels)

If the goods you are exporting are neither bulky nor heavy, it may be preferable to send them by air parcel post directly to the customers. The procedure is simple: you complete the appropriate customs declaration forms (obtainable from the post office) and hand them in when posting the parcel in the usual way. Your payment terms could be CBD (cash before delivery) or COD (cash on delivery).

Every country has its own regulations as to customs declaration forms, packing and prohibited goods. All this information is contained in the *Post Office Guide* which can be consulted at any post office or bought for £1 from main post offices. Other information is available from your local representative of the International Parcels division of the Post Office.

calculating your prices

In order to calculate the price to your customer abroad, you must have the following items of information:

○ the amount of any discounts for cash or quantity that your supplier will allow you (unless you are exporting your own goods)
○ any on-costs for export packing
○ cost of freight and transportation expenses; your forwarding agent will calculate these for you
○ bank charges; imposed by the bank through which you receive payment (between $\frac{1}{8}$ per cent and $\frac{1}{4}$ per cent of the total invoice value)
○ any costs for currency exchange
○ insurance cost for CIP quotations; you must also allow for the cost of insurance for the goods in transit from the works,

factory or store in this country to the docks if this is not included in the supplier's price; in some cases you may need a seller's interest policy even for an f.o.b. quote; you may need to add an ECGD premium

○ commission for your agent abroad, if you have one

○ your own profit.

insurance

You will need to find a reputable insurance company, probably through an insurance broker, to insure all your shipments. The insurers should supply you with a list of tariffs for different countries and types of risk. They will require information about each individual consignment, and will then quote accordingly. Some middle eastern countries have their own insurance companies, and ask for the goods to be shipped DCP only.

A consignment is generally insured up to the moment it is claimed by the consignee, including any time spent in a warehouse overseas: but, because of the high risk of pilferage, insurance companies may refuse to insure cargoes bound for some destinations beyond the time of arrival.

payment for exports

Commonly employed methods of payment are:

cash with order/cash before delivery

This is the most desirable method. You may not get it, but you can always ask.

documentary letter of credit

With this method, the exporter receives payment from a bank after presenting a complete set of documents *precisely* conforming to the requirements of the credit.

The customer, having accepted your quotation, opens a letter of credit in your favour: that is, he instructs his bank abroad to instruct a bank in Britain to pay you the agreed amount, on production of a correct and complete set of documents (hence 'documentary') and on satisfying any other agreed conditions.

There are several types of letter of credit (L/C for short). The most desirable is an irrevocable letter of credit confirmed (i.e., underwritten) by a recognised bank in Britain. Payment is guaranteed in all circumstances – revolution, currency crash, insolvency, act of God included. It is also the hardest to come by.

There are also unconfirmed irrevocable credits, the terms of which cannot be varied, save by agreement, and revocable letters of credit, which may facilitate payment, but are not secure.

forwarding documents

The complete set of documents required will be listed in the bank's advice of the credit, and may include:

- the original letter of credit
- the exporter's commercial invoice, signed (not the pro-forma, although it contains the same information)
- the bill of lading: 2 originals, endorsed in the form demanded by the bank, signed, dated and stamped 'shipped on board' by the shipping company, plus 3 or more non-negotiable copies; or a receipted air waybill.
- the insurance policy or certificate, in duplicate
- a set of two bills of exchange or a sight draft (which are a demand for payment)
- a certificate of origin, if required (issued and certified by the Chamber of Commerce) attesting that the goods are of UK origin
- export and import licences
- inspection certificates
- health certificates
- consular invoices.

All these documents must conform in every particular to the requirements of the letter of credit and to the customer's order with regard to the type and quantity of the goods, the marks (which identify the goods) and the measurements of the packing cases.

If there are any discrepancies, the bank is likely to withhold payment. And since the customers will be unable to claim the goods until the documents arrive at his end (forwarded by the bank), he may have to pay demurrage – the cost of storing them in a warehouse – for which he will want to be reimbursed by the exporter.

payment against documentary collection

This method should be used only with a tried and proven customer. He, in turn, must trust the exporter to supply goods of the exact type and quantity ordered: he undertakes to pay on a specified date (usually the arrival of the documents at the bank overseas or, in practice on the arrival of the goods at the destination). The terms of payment should be specified. If goods are exported without an explicit arrangement to an unknown or unreliable customer, the exporter may find himself in a situation where he has lost control of the goods without any certainty of receiving payment.

The same documents as for a letter of credit are required. The bank will release the documents to the customer (thus enabling him to claim the goods) when it has collected the payment.

payment by 30, 60 or 90 days drafts

This is a method which grants credit to the customer. It should be extended only to known customers in good financial standing. Before the customer can claim the documents, he must sign the drafts or bills of exchange, which you have issued, promising to pay the money due at some stated date – usually in 30, 60 or 90 days. The customer is then given the documents and can collect the goods – and sell them before having to pay for them. In EEC countries, some banks will avalise (guarantee) payment by their customers of bills of exchange.

Since you will receive your money with some delay, a reasonable allowance for interest should have been included in the price. Before quoting payment terms which do not guarantee payment, always check the credit rating of your customer, and use debt collectors if you are not paid in a reasonable time.

protection against export risks

The Export Credits Guarantee Department (ECGD), is a government department designed to protect the exporter against some of the hazards of trading overseas. It provides a specialised form of credit insurance (a form of insurance not normally covered by other insurers) for the UK exporter.

Its policies cover insolvency, default, considerable transfer delays, new restrictions imposed on imports by the government of the country and other risks. Up to 90 or 95 per cent of any risk is covered.

Your application to ECGD should be made on a proposal form obtainable from one of the nine ECGD regional offices. After a policy has been issued, ECGD will consider your individual applications for credit limits for particular customers overseas. It is also wise to discuss your credit insurance needs with the international division of your bank.

There are several types of ECGD policies giving cover from the date of contract or from the date of shipment. The premiums vary accordingly.

In the case of a claim, you must immediately get in touch with your ECGD office, and submit the following documentation:

○ a summary of the circumstances giving rise to the loss;
○ the buyer's orders and your confirmation of them;
○ the invoices;
○ evidence of despatch (e.g. carrier's receipt);
○ advice of acceptance of any bills of exchange and non-payment of them;
○ correspondence relating to the debt and all attempts to recover it;
○ statement of buyer's account to date for the two years prior to the despatch of the items forming the basis of the claim;
○ the information on which the buyer's creditworthiness was judged;
○ evidence of insolvency (if applicable).

exporting through confirming houses
Some British export houses (confirming houses) act on behalf of overseas customers. Instead of dealing with the ultimate customer, the exporter deals with the confirming house, and presents the usual shipping documents to it. The ECGD can give insurance for such transactions if there is any giving of export credit involved.

Some confirming houses charge the exporter a small commission for their services, others are paid by the customer.

some useful addresses for exporters
▲ Association of British Chambers of Commerce, 212a Shaftesbury Avenue, London WC2H 8EW (telephone: 01-240 5831)
▲ British Export Houses Association, 69 Cannon Street, London EC4N 5AB (telephone: 01-248 4444)
▲ British Overseas Trade Board, 1 Victoria Street, London SW1H 0ET (telephone: 01-215 7877) – also ten regional offices throughout the UK
▲ Croner Publications, Croner House, 173 Kingston Road, New Malden, Surrey KT3 3SS (telephone: 01-942 8966)
▲ Export Credits Guarantee Department, PO Box 272, Export House, 50 Ludgate Hill, London EC4M 7AY (telephone: 01-382 7000)
▲ ICC United Kingdom International Chamber of Commerce, Centre Point, 103 New Oxford Street, London WC1A 1QB (telephone: 01-240 5558).
▲ Institute of Export, Export House, 64 Clifton Street, London EC2A 4HB (telephone: 01-247 9812)
▲ Institute of Freight Forwarders, Suffield House, 9 Paradise Road, Richmond, Surrey TW9 1SA (telephone: 01-948 3141)
▲ SITPRO (Simplification of International Trade Procedures Board), Almack House, 26/28 King Street, London SW1Y 6QW (telephone: 01-930 0532).

BANKRUPTCY

If your financial position deteriorates so much that you are unable to pay your unsecured debts, or where it appears that there is no reasonable prospect that you will be able to pay a debt in the future, when it falls due for payment, a creditor may, if you owe him more than £750, bring bankruptcy proceedings against you. Two or more creditors may act jointly.

The creditor has to serve on you a formal demand, requiring you

○ to pay the debt, or
○ to give security for it, or
○ to compound for the petition debt: in other words, to propose an arrangements with the petitioning creditor, so that the debt can be paid off under an agreed scheme of payments.

If the debt is a future debt, the demand will require you to establish to the reasonable satisfaction of the creditor that you will be able to pay the debt when it falls due.

If you do not comply with the demand, or make an application to a bankruptcy court (the High Court in London or certain specified county courts) to set aside the demand (for example on the grounds that the money is not due, or that you have a claim against the creditor that equals or exceeds your debt to him), the creditor may, after the expiration of twenty-one days (or even earlier in exceptional cases) file a bankruptcy petition in a bankruptcy court.

The bankruptcy petition will be endorsed with the day and time for the hearing, and must be served on you.

The court has a discretion whether or not to make a bankruptcy order on the petition but will probably do so unless you

○ have paid off the debt
○ can show that the debt is not due
○ can show that there are sums owed to you by the creditor, which equal or exceed the debt due to him

o can show that you have made a proposal to compound or secure the debt, and that the creditor has unreasonably refused such proposal
o if the debt is a future debt, can satisfy the court that there is a reasonable prospect that you will be able to pay the debt when it falls due.

The court has power to adjourn or stay the petition, and might do so to enable you to make proposals to secure or compound the debt, or to pay it off, possibly by instalments. The court has a duty to protect the interest of all creditors and the public generally, and it may well not adjourn or stay the petition unless it is satisfied that you could deal not only with the petitioning creditor's debt but also with all your other unsecured debts.

avoiding bankruptcy proceedings
If you are in a situation where you cannot pay your debts in full, you may prefer to take steps yourself rather than allow a creditor to start bankruptcy proceedings against you.

One step would be to write informally to all your creditors, asking them to agree to accept payments according to a schedule agreed with them all. This has the advantage of cheapness, but will only work if all your creditors agree, and still leaves you liable to bankruptcy proceedings if any one of them changes his mind.

administration order
If your debts are less than £5000 and there is a county court judgment for at least one of the debts, you can apply to that court for an administration order to be made. Such an order will provide for all your debts (whether or not there are court orders relating to them) to be paid by single weekly or monthly payments to the court. The court will accumulate the payments and distribute them to your creditors pro rata, from time to time. Provided that you keep up such payments, no steps can be taken to enforce the debts by other means.

If you have no prospect of paying off all your debts within a reasonable time, the court can, on your application, order that you pay only a limited percentage of your debts.

voluntary arrangement with creditors

The Insolvency Act 1986 provides for voluntary arrangements to be made with your creditors, by enabling you to apply for approval of a composition or scheme whereby your debts are paid off by regular payments to an insolvency practitioner. He has to be appointed by the creditors, but you are responsible for paying him. He will distribute the payments among your creditors.

The first step is to apply to a bankruptcy court for an interim order which, if made, prevents any bankruptcy proceedings being taken against you or without the leave of the courts, or any other steps taken to enforce the judgment for a period of fourteen days (which can be extended). The insolvency practitioner has to enquire into your debts and consider whether a meeting of your creditors should be called to decide whether to agree to your proposals as to payment. If he considers that such a meeting is worth while, he is responsible for calling the meeting. The creditors who come to the meeting decide whether or not to accept your scheme. If it is accepted, that decision binds any creditor who had notice of and was entitled to attend that meeting. You must then carry out your part of the scheme by making regular payments as agreed.

If your creditors do not approve the scheme, then the interim order will lapse and any creditors can take steps to enforce the debt or start bankruptcy proceedings.

own bankruptcy petition

Finally, you may present your own petition in bankruptcy. Such a petition must be accompanied by a statement of your affairs, with details of all your debts and assets. Where your unsecured debts are less than £20,000 and your assets total at least £2,000, the court will not normally make an immediate bankruptcy order, but may appoint an insolvency practitioner to report on a possible voluntary arrangement with creditors, if it appears appropriate to the court to do so. Where a bankruptcy order is made, a certificate of summary administration will only be issued where on the hearing of a debtor's petition it appears to the court that the unsecured liabilities are less than £20,000 and that within the period of five years ending with the presentation of the petition, the debtor has neither been adjudged bankrupt, nor made a composition with his creditors in satisfaction of his debts, or a scheme of arrangement of his affairs.

effect of bankruptcy order

The effect of a bankruptcy order is that all your assets (subject to very limited exceptions) are vested in your trustee in bankruptcy on his appointment, and until then come under the control of the official receiver in bankruptcy. Your assets include your dwelling-house, and the trustee can seek an order for possession (if it is owned solely by you) or possession and sale (if it is owned jointly). The court must take into account the rights of your spouse under the Matrimonial Homes Act 1983 in considering whether or not to make such an order, but once one year has elapsed from the date of the trustee's appointment, the court assumes (save in exceptional circumstances) that the rights of the creditors outweigh all other considerations.

Unless you have been bankrupt previously or the court otherwise orders, a bankruptcy order lasts three years (two years in the case of a certificate of summary administration) and you are then discharged from the disabilities of a bankrupt.

On discharge, your assets remain vested in your trustee, who is able to sell them to pay off your debts and they remain so vested in him until all your debts are paid in full and the bankruptcy order is annulled.

Although the discharge releases you from most of your bankruptcy debts, you remain liable for certain debts including any judgment for damages arising out of an action in negligence for personal injury, and any court orders in family proceedings.

During the course of your bankruptcy you have a duty to complete a statement of affairs, giving full details of your debts and assets and also to assist the official receiver and your trustee in ascertaining your assets and getting them in. You may be required to attend a public examination, at which you will be questioned about the reasons for your insolvency and your dealing with assets. Your trustee may apply to the court for an order requiring you to make regular payments out of your income towards payment of your debts.

Under the Insolvency Act 1986, it is a criminal offence not to have kept proper accounting records of your business from a date two years prior to the presentation of the petition in bankruptcy, up to the date of the bankruptcy order or, having kept such books, not to have preserved them. The accounting records must be such as will show and explain the transactions of your business, and must include records of all cash received and paid; and, where the business deals in goods, there must be statements of annual stocktaking, and accounts of all goods sold and bought, showing (except for retail sales) the names of buyers and sellers. It is also an offence if, during the same period, you have materially contributed to or increased the extent of your insolvency by gambling or rash and hazardous speculation.

The principal disabilities of a bankrupt are that he commits an offence if he obtains credit for more than £250 without disclosing the bankruptcy; or engages in business under a name other than that in which he was made bankrupt, without disclosing to the people with whom he is trading, the name in which he was made bankrupt.

▲ You can obtain a *Guide to Bankruptcy Law* from the Insolvency Service, 2–14 Bunhill Row, London EC1Y 8LL (telephone: 01-606 4071 extension 3117).

LOOKING TO THE FUTURE

This book has been about starting a business. The question of making it expand, and even proliferate, would need another book to itself. But there are some things to consider when you begin looking ahead and making long-term plans.

changing the firm's status
If you started trading as a sole trader or partnership, you might consider changing the status of your business to that of a private limited company. This is a matter for periodic review, so perhaps you should add it to the agenda for your yearly general discussion with your accountant.

The chief advantage of this change would be to limit your liability (and your partners' liability, too, of course); it might also make it easier for you to raise finance. On the other hand, as the director of a limited company, you would not be able to set off the company's trading losses against your own income. You may also find that your bank, your other lenders and your major suppliers may ask for a director's personal guarantee.

If you do decide on this move, make sure that you time it to your best advantage from the tax point of view, after consultation with your accountant. One indication (but only one factor amongst many) that a change of status might be a tax advantage, could be that your profits (when combined with your spouse's income) are giving you a taxable income of round about £30,000–£35,000.

delegating responsibility
If yours is a manufacturing business, even if you have started off by doing everything yourself, you will probably discover that you must save yourself for the more responsible aspects of your work, and find someone else to take over the more routine tasks. The next step might be to divide the major responsibilities with

another person: one to concentrate on the technical side, while the other one attends to the marketing and sales.

One possibility is taking on a partner or co-director with the qualifications you require, who would also be prepared to invest money in the business. This would bring a triple benefit: help in management, extra finance, and a newcomer with the incentive to work hard.

A personal recommendation from a knowledgeable person, such as your accountant, may be a way to find such a person; or by advertising in your trade press, clearly setting out your requirements, and what you have to offer.

Ask all applicants for personal and bank references (and take them up by personal contact with the referee). Agree a trial period with your chosen applicant, at the end of which either party will be entitled to call it a day if the arrangement is found to be unsatisfactory.

Before clinching the deal, agree with your new colleague the maximum amount that each of you will draw as salary, at least in the first year or two. It would be pointless to have a partner who insisted on withdrawing his whole investment in the form of his first year's salary.

As your business grows, some of your original employees will be promoted to positions of greater responsibility. They will have become experienced in your business, they will know and may be known to your customers, so there is the risk that they might leave and set up on their own, perhaps even in the same area, taking away much of your business.

There is no complete protection against this – perhaps you yourself got your start in the same way? Nevertheless, when you promote an employee, and so revise his job description, you may be able to introduce some safeguards: a longer period of notice, for instance, and other precautions which a lawyer might be able to suggest to you.

to expand or not?

Expansion means different things to different people. For the smallest firms, taking on one full-time employee may double the workforce, while for others which cannot get off the ground without a considerable staff, the notion of expansion is far more impressive. But in both cases the motivation is the same: greater profits.

One firm may seek to increase profits by trying for a greater turnover, with the existing range of products, another firm may look for ways to increase current profit margins, both confident that the demand for their product will continue. A third firm, having less confidence, will try to increase profits through developing new products within the same industry, or through diversifying into other, possibly unrelated, industries.

Whichever way you choose, the same considerations apply as in starting up: you must plan ahead, time your actions accurately, and make sure well in advance that you have the necessary financial backing, and beware of overtrading. Many firms come to grief by attempting to expand in excess of their financial resources.

sub-contracting work
If in your case expansion means increasing your production, and your factory is already working to capacity, do not be in too much of a hurry to acquire new work space, plant and labour: you could be in serious trouble if there were to be a falling-off of trade. Instead, consider whether there is some part of your manufacturing process which could be turned over to a sub-contractor, which would ease the pressure of work, giving you time to plan what to do next.

If the part you want to sub-contract is a relatively simple operation, consider the possibility of handing it over to a youth training workshop or a sheltered workshop: there is likely to be one or more of each sort in your area.

In using such workshops, you are not only doing a social service, but perhaps training up future employees for your firm.

moving to larger premises
Think hard before taking on larger premises: additional space means additional overheads costs, and will inevitably increase

your working capital requirements. Think whether you could manage with the space you have, through cleverer deployment of plant and equipment, or a more logical arrangement of the work sequence. It might be worthwhile calling in an expert on factory planning or work study, to advise you on this.

If you take on premises with room for growth, mark off the spare space and be ruthless about not allowing it to be used until the growth in production demands and justifies it. It is all too easy to fill up all available space with no compensating growth in turnover.

organisations that can help you

If you have become disheartened by the thought of the many laws and regulations that you must obey, you might consider joining the Alliance of Small Firms and Self-employed People (ASP), 33 The Green, Calne, Wiltshire SN11 8DJ (telephone: 0249-817003). It publishes a quarterly journal, *Business Informer*, which gives updating information on taxation and employment. There is a legal-expenses insurance scheme which members can join. The ASP tries to bring pressure to bear on the government to reduce the legislative burden on small businesses, and has a team of advisers who can help members with specific problems arising from bureaucracy or legislation.

Once you have established your business, set up a company or partnership, you should consider joining the Association of Independent Businesses. This is run by practising businessmen, with the aim of improving the political and financial climate for the privately owned business. In addition to its lobbying role, it offers members an 'Adviceline' which covers most of the problems facing the smaller firm. It also offers discounts on health insurance and vehicle purchase.

Subscriptions start at £25 a year for an individual and one or two employees. The national office of the AIB is at Trowbray House, 108 Weston Street, London SE1 3QB (telephone: 01-403 4066), with 11 regional councils and five political committees: the AIB does not support any one political party.

. . . a last thought

Every so often – say once a month – stop thinking about the day to day problems and consider what you are really trying to achieve: what you have already achieved so far and what needs doing to get you to your next goal. You have a better chance of arriving if you know your destination beforehand.

INDEX

CONSUMER PUBLICATIONS

The list of CA's Consumer Publications includes:

Earning money at home

Living with stress

The legal side of buying a house (England and Wales)

Wills and probate

What to do when someone dies

Which? way to buy, sell and move house

Children, parents and the law

Divorce, legal procedures and financial facts

Renting and letting

Taking your own case to court or tribunal

Understanding cancer

Avoiding heart trouble

What will my pension be?

Approaching retirement

Living through middle age

The Which? book of insurance

CONSUMER PUBLICATIONS are available from
Consumers' Association, Castlemead, Gascoyne Way, Hertford
SG14 1LH and from booksellers.